Interactive Reader and St

Holt Social Studies

World History

HOLT, RINEHART AND WINSTON

A Harcourt Education Company

Orlando • **Austin** • New York • San Diego • Toronto • London

ISBN 0-03-042314-7

7 8 9   018   09 08 07

Contents

Contents

Contents

How to Use This Book

The Interactive Reader and Study Guide was developed to help you get the most from your world history course. Using this book will help you master the content of the course while developing your reading and vocabulary skills. Reviewing the next few pages before getting started will make you aware of the many useful features of this book.

Chapter Summary pages help you connect with the big picture. Studying them will keep you focused on the information you will need to be successful on your exams.

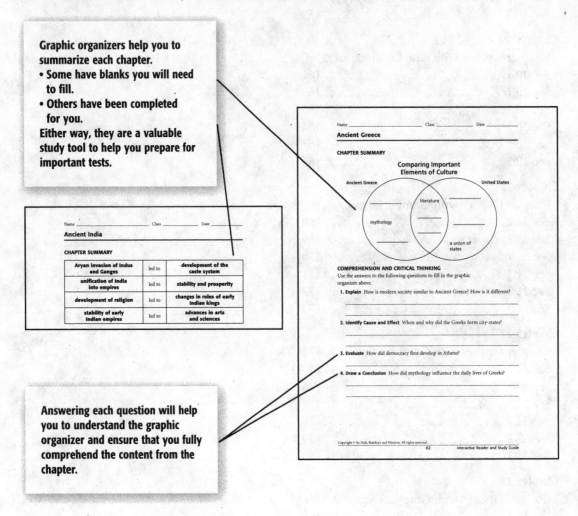

Graphic organizers help you to summarize each chapter.
- **Some have blanks you will need to fill.**
- **Others have been completed for you.**

Either way, they are a valuable study tool to help you prepare for important tests.

Answering each question will help you to understand the graphic organizer and ensure that you fully comprehend the content from the chapter.

Section Summary pages allow you to interact easily with the content and Key Terms from each section.

Main Ideas statements from your textbook focus your attention as you read the summaries.

Clearly labeled page headers make navigating the book extraordinarily simple.

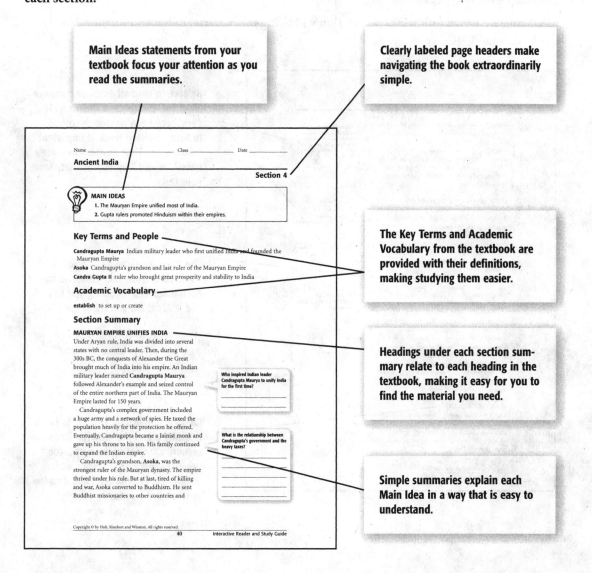

Name _____ Class _____ Date _____

Ancient India

Section 4

💡 **MAIN IDEAS**
1. The Mauryan Empire unified most of India.
2. Gupta rulers promoted Hinduism within their empires.

Key Terms and People

Candragupta Maurya Indian military leader who first unified India and founded the Mauryan Empire
Asoka Candragupta's grandson and last ruler of the Mauryan Empire
Candra Gupta II ruler who brought great prosperity and stability to India

Academic Vocabulary

establish to set up or create

Section Summary

MAURYAN EMPIRE UNIFIES INDIA
Under Aryan rule, India was divided into several states with no central leader. Then, during the 300s BC, the conquests of Alexander the Great brought much of India into his empire. An Indian military leader named **Candragupta Maurya** followed Alexander's example and seized control of the entire northern part of India. The Mauryan Empire lasted for 150 years.

Candragupta's complex government included a huge army and a network of spies. He taxed the population heavily for the protection he offered. Eventually, Candragupta became a Jainist monk and gave up his throne to his son. His family continued to expand the Indian empire.

Candragupta's grandson, **Asoka**, was the strongest ruler of the Mauryan dynasty. The empire thrived under his rule. But at last, tired of killing and war, Asoka converted to Buddhism. He sent Buddhist missionaries to other countries and

Who inspired Indian leader Candragupta Maurya to unify India for the first time?
_____
_____
_____

What is the relationship between Candragupta's government and the heavy taxes?
_____
_____
_____

The Key Terms and Academic Vocabulary from the textbook are provided with their definitions, making studying them easier.

Headings under each section summary relate to each heading in the textbook, making it easy for you to find the material you need.

Simple summaries explain each Main Idea in a way that is easy to understand.

Notes throughout the margins help you to interact with the content and understand the information you are reading.

Challenge Activities following each section will bring the material to life and further develop your analysis skills.

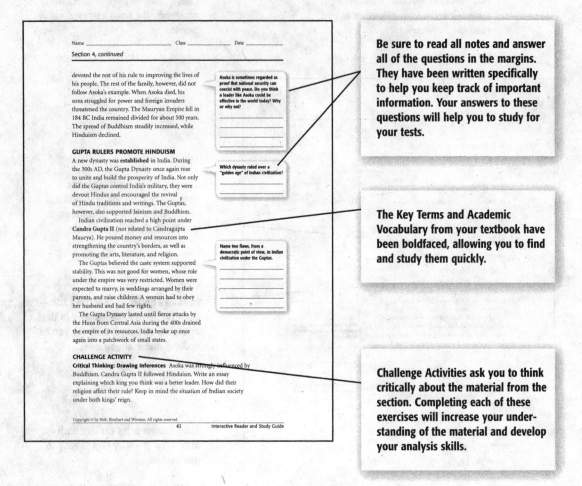

Name _____ Class _____ Date _____

Section 4, *continued*

devoted the rest of his rule to improving the lives of his people. The rest of the family, however, did not follow Asoka's example. When Asoka died, his sons struggled for power and foreign invaders threatened the country. The Mauryan Empire fell in 184 BC India remained divided for about 500 years. The spread of Buddhism steadily increased, while Hinduism declined.

GUPTA RULERS PROMOTE HINDUISM

A new dynasty was **established** in India. During the 300s AD, the Gupta Dynasty once again rose to unite and build the prosperity of India. Not only did the Guptas control India's military, they were devout Hindus and encouraged the revival of Hindu traditions and writings. The Guptas, however, also supported Jainism and Buddhism.

Indian civilization reached a high point under **Candra Gupta II** (not related to Candragupta Maurya). He poured money and resources into strengthening the country's borders, as well as promoting the arts, literature, and religion.

The Guptas believed the caste system supported stability. This was not good for women, whose role under the empire was very restricted. Women were expected to marry, in weddings arranged by their parents, and raise children. A woman had to obey her husband and had few rights.

The Gupta Dynasty lasted until fierce attacks by the Huns from Central Asia during the 400s drained the empire of its resources. India broke up once again into a patchwork of small states.

CHALLENGE ACTIVITY

Critical Thinking: Drawing Inferences Asoka was strongly influenced by Buddhism. Candra Gupta II followed Hinduism. Write an essay explaining which king you think was a better leader. How did their religion affect their rule? Keep in mind the situation of Indian society under both kings' reign.

Asoka is sometimes regarded as proof that national security can coexist with peace. Do you think a leader like Asoka could be effective in the world today? Why or why not?

Which dynasty ruled over a "golden age" of Indian civilization?

Name two flaws, from a democratic point of view, in Indian civilization under the Guptas.

Copyright © by Holt, Rinehart and Winston. All rights reserved.

41   Interactive Reader and Study Guide

Be sure to read all notes and answer all of the questions in the margins. They have been written specifically to help you keep track of important information. Your answers to these questions will help you to study for your tests.

The Key Terms and Academic Vocabulary from your textbook have been boldfaced, allowing you to find and study them quickly.

Challenge Activities ask you to think critically about the material from the section. Completing each of these exercises will increase your understanding of the material and develop your analysis skills.

Uncovering the Past

CHAPTER SUMMARY

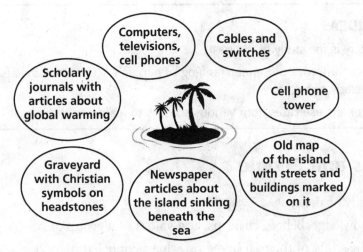

COMPREHENSION AND CRITICAL THINKING

Use information from the graphic organizer to answer the following questions.

1. Explain Did people live on this island before the water covered it?

_____

_____

2. Draw Inferences What was most likely the predominant religion among the people who lived on this island?

_____

_____

3. Identify Cause and Effect What global climatic phenomenon caused the water to rise and cover the island?

_____

_____

4. Evaluate Was the civilization of the island technically advanced?

_____

_____

_____

Uncovering the Past

MAIN IDEAS
1. History is the study of the past.
2. We can improve our understanding of people's actions and beliefs through the study of history.
3. Historians use clues from various sources to learn about the past.

Key Terms and People

history the study of the past

culture the knowledge, beliefs, customs, and values of a group of people

archaeology the study of the past based on what people left behind

fossil a part or imprint of something that was once alive

artifacts objects created by and used by humans

primary source an account of an event created by someone who took part in or witnessed the event

secondary source information gathered by someone who did not take part in or witness an event

Academic Vocabulary

values ideas that people hold dear and try to live by

Section Summary

THE STUDY OF THE PAST

History is the study of the past. Historians are people who study history. Historians want to know how people lived and why they did the things they did. They try to learn about the problems people faced and how they found solutions. They are interested in how people lived their daily lives. They study the past to understand people's culture. **Culture** is the knowledge, beliefs, customs, and values of a group of people.

The study of the past based on what people left behind is called **archaeology** (ahr-kee-AH-luh-jee).

> What do we call people who study how people lived in the past?
>
> _____
>
> _____

Section 1, continued

Archaeologists explore places where people once lived, worked, or fought. They examine the things that people left in these places to learn what they can tell about the past.

> How can studying history teach you about yourself?
>
> _____
>
> _____
>
> _____

UNDERSTANDING THROUGH HISTORY

Understanding the past helps you understand the world today. History can even teach you about yourself. What if you did not know about your own past? You would not know what makes you proud about yourself. You would not know what mistakes you should not repeat.

History is just as important for groups. What would happen if countries had no record of their past? People would not remember their nation's great triumphs or tragedies. History shapes our identity and teaches us the **values** that we share.

History also teaches about cultures that are unlike your own. Learning other people's stories can help you respect and understand different opinions. You also learn to understand how today's events are shaped by events of the past. History encourages you to ask important questions.

> Circle the sentence that explains why history helps you relate more easily to people of different backgrounds.

USING CLUES

We learn about history from a variety of sources. **Fossils**, such as bones or footprints preserved in rock, give us clues to life very long ago. **Artifacts**, such as tools, coins, or pottery, also give us information. Writing has taught us a great deal. Writing can be a **primary source** (by someone who took part in or witnessed an event) or a **secondary source** (information gathered by someone who did not take part in or witness an event).

> What sources give us clues to life very long ago?
>
> _____
>
> _____
>
> _____

CHALLENGE ACTIVITY

Critical Thinking: Drawing Inferences Imagine a tribe or group of people that might have lived a long time ago. Write a short essay about their culture.

Interactive Reader and Study Guide

Section 2

> **MAIN IDEAS**
> 1. Geography is the study of places and people.
> 2. Studying location is important to both physical and human geography.
> 3. Geography and history are closely connected.

Key Terms and People

geography the study of the earth's physical and cultural features

environment all the living and nonliving things that affect life in an area

landforms the natural features of the land's surface

climate the pattern of weather conditions in a certain area over a long period of time

region an area with one or more features that make it different from surrounding areas

resources materials found in the earth that people need and value

Academic Vocabulary

features characteristics

Section Summary

STUDYING PLACES AND PEOPLE

To understand what happened in the past, you need to know where events took place and who was involved. That is why historians study the earth's physical and cultural **features**, such as mountains, rivers, people, cities, and countries. This study is called **geography**.

Geography has two main areas of study. Physical geography is the study of the earth's land and features. Human geography is the study of people and the places where they live. Physical geographers study the **environment**, which includes all the living and nonliving things that affect life in an area. The most important features for physical geographers are **landforms**, the natural features of

> What subject helps historians to understand where events took place?
>
> _____
>
> _____

> What are the two main areas of study in geography?
>
> _____
>
> _____
>
> _____

the land's surface. Physical geographers also study **climate**, the weather conditions in a certain area over a long period of time. Specialists in human geography study many interesting questions about how people and the environment affect each other.

> **What is climate?**
> _____
> _____
> _____

STUDYING LOCATION

No two places are exactly alike. That is why geographers try to understand how different locations can affect human populations, or groups of people. Geographers use maps to study and compare locations. A map is a drawing of an area. Some maps show physical features, such as mountains, forests, and rivers. Other maps show cities and the boundaries of states or countries. Studying location is often helped by learning about **regions**, or areas with one or more features that make them different from surrounding areas.

> **What is the main tool that geographers use to study and compare locations?**
> _____
> _____

GEOGRAPHY AND HISTORY

Geography gives us important clues about the people and places that came before us. Like detectives, we can piece together a great deal of information about past cultures by knowing where people lived and what the area was like.

Early people settled in places that were rich in resources. **Resources** are materials that are found in the earth that people need and value. Resources include water, animals, land for farming, stone for tools, and metals. Features and resources influence the development of cultures and the growth of civilizations. The relationship between geography and people is not one sided. People influence their environments in both positive and negative ways.

> **Underline the sentence that explains how geography gives us clues about the past.**

CHALLENGE ACTIVITY

Critical Thinking: Drawing Inferences Draw a map of an imaginary country or region. Include features such as mountains, rivers, and cities.

Interactive Reader and Study Guide

The Stone Ages and Early Cultures

CHAPTER SUMMARY

Need for food	led to	development of tools
Changes in climate patterns	led to	migrations
Need to communicate	led to	development of language
Farming communities	led to	growth of towns

COMPREHENSION AND CRITICAL THINKING

Use information from the graphic organizer to answer the following questions.

1. Explain What were the earliest stone tools used for?

_____

_____

2. Identify Cause and Effect Why did so many people migrate during the ice ages?

_____

_____

3. Evaluate Why did hunter-gatherer societies develop language?

_____

4. Draw a Conclusion How did farming contribute to the growth of towns?

_____

_____

The Stone Ages and Early Cultures

MAIN IDEAS

1. Scientists study the remains of early humans to learn about prehistory.
2. Hominids and early humans first appeared in East Africa millions of years ago.
3. Stone Age tools grew more complex as time passed.
4. Hunter-gatherer societies developed language, art, and religion.

Key Terms and People

prehistory the time before there was writing

hominid an early ancestor of humans

ancestor a relative who lived in the past

tool any handheld object that has been modified to help a person accomplish a task

Paleolithic Era the first part of the Stone Age

hunter-gatherers people who hunt animals and gather wild plants, seeds, fruits, and nuts to survive

society a community of people who share a common culture

Academic Vocabulary

distribute to divide among a group of people

Section Summary

SCIENTISTS STUDY REMAINS

Although humans have lived on the earth for more than a million years, writing was not invented until about 5,000 years ago. Historians call the time before there was writing **prehistory**. To study prehistory, historians rely on the work of archaeologists and anthropologists.

Archaeologists have found old bones that appear to belong to **hominids**, early **ancestors** of humans. Discoveries of ancient bones give us information about early humans and their ancestors, but not all scientists agree on the meaning of these discoveries.

> What do historians call the time before there was writing?
>
> _____
>
> _____

> Do you think that hominids are the same as humans, or did they come before humans?

HOMINIDS AND EARLY HUMANS

As time passed hominids became more like modern humans. Many scientists think that the first modern humans appeared in Africa about 200,000 years ago. Scientists call these early humans *homo sapiens*, or "wise man." Every person alive today belongs to this group.

> What do scientists call modern humans?
> _____
> _____

STONE AGE TOOLS

During the **Paleolithic** (pay-lee-uh-LI-thik) **Era**, which lasted until about 10,000 years ago, people used sharpened stones as **tools**. Stone tools were probably used to cut, chop, and scrape roots, bones, or meat. Later, people learned how to attach wooden handles to sharp stones to make hand axes and spears.

> Can you think of an advantage to attaching a wooden handle to a stone tool? Draw a picture if it will help you visualize the tool.

HUNTER-GATHERER SOCIETIES

Anthropologists believe that early humans lived in small groups of **hunter-gatherers**. In these **societies**, men hunted and women collected plants to eat and took care of children. These societies developed cultures with language, religion, and art. Language developed as a means of communicating and of resolving issues like how to **distribute** food.

> What cultural element did Stone Age societies develop as a means of communicating and resolving issues?
> _____
> _____

CHALLENGE ACTIVITY

Critical Thinking: Drawing Inferences Many years from now, an archaeologist discovers your house with nothing in it but old furniture, appliances, tools, and bits of clothing. Write a short essay describing some conclusions the archaeologist might draw from these artifacts.

The Stone Ages and Early Cultures

Section 2

MAIN IDEAS

1. People moved out of Africa as the earth's climates changed.
2. People adapted to new environments by making clothing and new types of tools.

Key Terms and People

ice ages long periods of freezing weather

migrate move to a new place

land bridge a strip of land connecting two continents

Mesolithic Era the middle part of the Stone Age, from about 10,000 years ago to about 5,000 years ago

Section Summary

PEOPLE MOVE OUT OF AFRICA

About 1.6 million years ago, many places around the world began to experience **ice ages**, or long periods of freezing weather. In response to these changes, many hominids and early humans **migrated** from Africa to Asia and eventually spread to India, China, Southeast Asia, and Europe. The ice ages ended about 10,000 years ago.

During the ice ages, huge sheets of ice covered much of the earth's land. These ice sheets were formed from ocean water, leaving ocean levels lower than they are now. Many areas that are now under water were dry land then. Scientists think that in some places the ocean level dropped and exposed **land bridges** between continents. These land bridges allowed Stone Age people to migrate around the world. Early humans probably came to North America across a land bridge from northern Asia, and spread throughout North America and to South America. By 9000 BC, humans lived on all continents except Antarctica.

> Use the library or an online resource to find a map showing the approximate dates and routes of early human migrations.

> From which continent did the first early humans probably come to North America?
>
> _____
> _____

PEOPLE ADAPT TO NEW ENVIRONMENTS

Early people had to learn to adapt to new environments. The places to which they migrated were often much colder than the places they left, and often had strange plants and animals.

To keep warm, they learned to sew animal skins together to make clothing. At first they took shelter in caves. When they moved to areas with no caves, they built their own shelters. At first these shelters were pits in the ground with roofs of branches and leaves. Later, people learned to build more permanent structures with wood, stone, clay, or other materials, even bones from large animals such as mammoths. They covered frames with animal hides to form solid roofs and walls.

> **What materials did early humans use to cover frame structures with roofs and walls?**
> _____
> _____

People also began to make new types of tools. These tools were smaller and more complex than tools from the Paleolithic Era. They defined the **Mesolithic** (me-zuh-LI-thik) **Era**, which began more than 10,000 years ago and lasted to about 5,000 years ago in some places. These new tools included hooks and spears for fishing, and bows and arrows for hunting.

People in the Mesolithic Era also developed new technologies to improve their lives. For example, they learned how to make pots from clay, how to hollow out logs to make canoes, and how to use dogs for protection and to help them hunt.

> **How did early humans make canoes?**
> _____
> _____
> _____

CHALLENGE ACTIVITY

Critical Thinking: Drawing Inferences Draw a building plan with written instructions for a Mesolithic dwelling.

The Stone Ages and Early Cultures

Section 3

> **MAIN IDEAS**
> 1. The first farmers learned to grow plants and raise animals in the Stone Age.
> 2. Farming changed societies and the way people lived.

Key Terms and People

Neolithic Era the last Stone Age, lasting from about 10,000 years ago to about 5,000 years ago in Egypt and Southwest Asia and later elsewhere

domestication the process of changing plants or animals to make them more useful to humans

agriculture the development of farming from the domestication of plants

megaliths huge stones used as monuments or sites for religious gatherings

Academic Vocabulary

development creation and growth

Section Summary

THE FIRST FARMERS

A warming trend brought an end to the ice ages, and new plants began to grow in some areas. As early as 10,000 years ago, in Egypt and Southwest Asia, people came to depend on wild barley and wheat for food. People soon learned that they could plant seeds to grow their own crops. This shift from food gathering to food producing defined the **Neolithic** (nee-uh-LI-thik) **Era.**

This **domestication** of plants led to the **development** of **agriculture**, or farming. The first farmers also learned to domesticate animals. Instead of following wild herds, they could now keep sheep and goats for milk, food, and wool. People could also use large animals like cattle to carry loads or to pull large tools used in farming. Domestication

> What brought an end to the ice ages?
> _____
> _____

> Use the library or an online resource to find a map showing where specific plants and animals were first domesticated.

greatly improved people's chances of surviving. With survival more certain, people could focus on activities other than finding food.

During this time, people also learned to polish stones to make specialized tools like saws and drills. People also learned how to make fire. Before learning that skill, peopel could use only fire that had been started by natural causes, such as lightning.

> **What great discovery did Neolithic people make about fire?**
> _____
> _____
> _____

FARMING CHANGES SOCIETIES

People began to make clothing from plant fibers and wool as well as from animal skins. As these early farmers learned to control their own food production and to make better shelters and clothing, populations grew. In some areas farming communities developed into towns.

> **What two materials were first used by Neolithic people to make clothing?**
> _____
> _____
> _____

Some groups gathered to perform religious ceremonies around huge stone monuments called **megaliths**. These people probably believed in gods and goddesses associated with the four elements— air, water, fire, and earth—or with animals. Some scholars believe that prehistoric people also prayed to their ancestors. Some societies today still hold these beliefs.

> **What are the four elements?**
> _____
> _____
> _____
> _____
> _____

CHALLENGE ACTIVITY

Critical Thinking: Drawing Inferences Use the Internet or a library to research theories about how the megaliths at Stonehenge in England were built. Then write your own theory.

Mesopotamia and the Fertile Crescent

CHAPTER SUMMARY

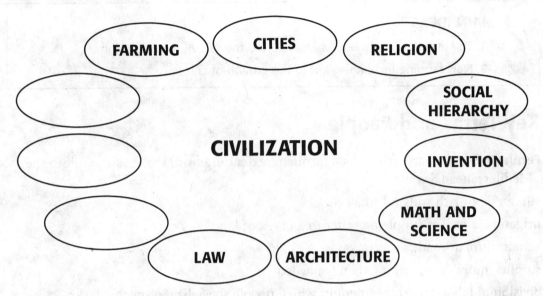

COMPREHENSION AND CRITICAL THINKING

Use information from the graphic organizer to answer the following questions.

1. **Identify** Which two of the eight aspects of civilization in the graphic organizer above can be classed as economic structures?

   _____

   _____

2. **Interpret** Of the following five words (ARTS, SILT, WRITING, TRADE, OIL), which three belong in the graphic organizer above? Write the three correct words in the empty circles.

3. **Sequence** Of the eleven words or phrases around the word CIVILIZATION, which comes first in time order? Which do you think comes last?

   _____

   _____

Mesopotamia and the Fertile Crescent

> **MAIN IDEAS**
> 1. The rivers of Southwest Asia supported the growth of civilization.
> 2. New farming techniques led to the growth of cities.

Key Terms and People

Fertile Crescent a large arc of rich farmland extending from the Persian Gulf to the Mediterranean Sea

silt a mix of rich soil and small rocks

irrigation a way of supplying water to an area of land

canals human-made waterways

surplus more of something than is needed

division of labor an arrangement in which people specialize in specific tasks

Section Summary

RIVERS SUPPORT THE GROWTH OF CIVILIZATION

Early people settled where crops would grow. Crops usually grew well near rivers, where water was available and regular floods made the soil rich.

Mesopotamia, part of the region known as the **Fertile Crescent** in Southwest Asia, lay between the Tigris and Euphrates rivers. Every year, floods on the rivers brought **silt**. The fertile silt made the land ideal for farming.

Hunter-gatherer groups first settled in Mesopotamia more than 12,000 years ago. Over time these people learned how to work together to control floods. They planted crops and grew their own food.

Farm settlements formed in Mesopotamia as early as 7000 BC. Farmers grew wheat, barley, and other grains. Livestock, birds, and fish were also sources of food. Plentiful food led to population growth and villages formed. Eventually, these early villages developed into the world's first civilization.

> "Mesopotamia" means "between the rivers" in Greek. To which two rivers does the name of the region refer?
>
> _____
> _____
> _____

> Name two grains grown by Mesopotamian farmers.
>
> _____
> _____
> _____

Interactive Reader and Study Guide

FARMING AND CITIES

Early farmers faced the challenge of learning how to control the flow of river water to their fields in both rainy and dry seasons. Flooding destroyed crops, killed livestock, and washed away homes. When water levels were too low, crops dried up.

> Underline the sentence that lists some of the problems caused by flooding.

To solve their problems, Mesopotamians used **irrigation**. They dug out large storage basins to hold water supplies. Then they dug **canals** that connected these basins to a network of ditches. These ditches brought water to the fields and watered grazing areas for cattle and sheep.

> From where did the water collected in the storage basins come?
> _____
> _____

Because irrigation made farmers more productive, they produced a **surplus**. Some people became free to do other jobs. For the first time, people became craftspersons, religious leaders, and government workers. A **division of labor** developed.

Mesopotamian settlements grew in size and complexity. Most people continued to work in farming jobs. However, cities became important places. People traded goods in cities. Cities became the political, religious, cultural, and economic centers of Mesopotamian civilization.

> Which places in Mesopotamia became the centers of civilization?
> _____
> _____

CHALLENGE ACTIVITY

Critical Thinking: Drawing Inferences Write a proposal for an irrigation system that will divert flood waters and benefit riverbank farmers.

Mesopotamia and the Fertile Crescent

MAIN IDEAS

1. The Sumerians created the world's first complex, advanced society.
2. Religion played a major role in Sumerian society.
3. Sumerian society was divided into classes.

Key Terms and People

rural having to do with the countryside

urban having to do with the city

city-state a political unit consisting of a city and the surrounding countryside

empire land with different territories and people under a single rule

polytheism the worship of many gods

priests people who performed religious ceremonies

social hierarchy a division of society by rank or class

Academic Vocabulary

role a part or function

Section Summary

AN ADVANCED SOCIETY

In southern Mesopotamia about 3000 BC, people known as the Sumerians (soo-MER-ee-unz) created a complex, advanced society. Most people in Sumer (soo-muhr) lived in **rural** areas, but they were governed from **urban** areas that controlled the surrounding countryside. The size of the countryside controlled by each of these **city-states** depended on its military strength. Stronger city-states controlled larger areas. Individual city-states gained and lost power over time.

Around 2300 BC Sargon was the leader of the Akkadians (uh-KAY-dee-uhns), a people who lived to the north of Sumer. Sargon built a large army

> Why do you think governments are usually located in cities?
>
> _____
> _____
> _____
> _____

and defeated all the city-states of Sumer as well as all of northern Mesopotamia. With these conquests, Sargon established the world's first **empire**. It stretched from the Persian Gulf to the Mediterranean Sea. The Akkadian empire lasted about 150 years.

> Use a world atlas to determine how many miles across the Akkadian empire extended.

RELIGION SHAPES SOCIETY

Religion played an important **role** in nearly every aspect of Sumerian public and private life. Sumerians practiced **polytheism**, the worship of many gods. They believed that their gods had enormous powers. Gods could bring a good harvest or a disastrous flood. The gods could bring illness or they could bring good health and wealth. The Sumerians believed that success in every area of life depended on pleasing the gods. Each city-state considered one god to be its special protector. People relied on **priests** to help them gain the gods' favor. Priests interpreted the wishes of the gods and made offerings to them.

> Do you think religion plays an important role in public life today? Why or why not?
>
> _____
> _____
> _____
> _____

A **social hierarchy** developed in Sumerian city-states. Kings were at the top. Below them were priests and nobles. The middle ranks included skilled craftspeople and merchants. Farmers and laborers made up the large working class. Slaves were at the bottom of the social order. Although the role of most women was limited to the home and raising children, some upper-class women were educated and even became priestesses.

> In Sumerian religious practice, what did priests do to try to please the gods?
>
> _____
> _____

> Which two groups formed the Sumerian upper classes?
>
> _____
> _____
> _____

CHALLENGE ACTIVITY

Critical Thinking: Drawing Inferences You are the king of a Sumerian city-state. Write a letter to your priests asking them to make offerings to the gods in order to protect your farms from a possible flood.

Mesopotamia and the Fertile Crescent

MAIN IDEAS

1. The Sumerians invented the world's first writing system.
2. Advances and inventions changed Sumerian lives.
3. Many types of art developed in Sumer.

Key Terms and People

cuneiform the Sumerian system of writing, which used symbols to represent basic parts of words

pictographs picture symbols that represented objects such as trees or animals

scribe writer

epics long poems that tell the story of a hero

architecture the science of building

ziggurat a pyramid-shaped temple tower

Section Summary

THE INVENTION OF WRITING

The Sumerians made one of the greatest cultural advances in history. They developed **cuneiform** (kyoo-NEE-uh-fohrm), the world's first system of writing. But Sumerians did not have pencils, pens, or paper. Instead, they used sharp reeds to make wedge-shaped symbols on clay tablets.

Sumerians first used cuneiform to keep records for business, government, and temples. As the use of cuneiform grew, simple **pictographs** evolved into more complex symbols that represented basic parts of words. Writing was taught in schools. Becoming a writer, or **scribe**, was a way to move up in social class. Scribes began to combine symbols to express complex ideas. In time, scribes wrote works on law, grammar, and mathematics. Sumerians also wrote stories, proverbs, songs, poems to celebrate military victories, and long poems called **epics**.

> Write the name of the world's first system of writing.
>
> _____
>
> _____

> What are pictographs?
>
> _____
>
> _____
>
> _____
>
> _____

Interactive Reader and Study Guide

ADVANCES AND INVENTIONS

The Sumerians were the first to build wheeled vehicles like carts and wagons. They invented the potter's wheel, a device that spins wet clay as a craftsperson shapes it into bowls. They invented the ox-drawn plow and greatly improved farm production. They built sewers under city streets. They learned to use bronze to make strong tools and weapons. They named thousands of animals, plants, and minerals, and used them to produce healing drugs. The clock and the calendar we use today are based on Sumerian methods of measuring time.

> **Which Sumerian invention greatly improved farm production?**
> _____
> _____

THE ARTS OF SUMER

Sumerian remains reveal great skill in **architecture**. A pyramid-shaped **ziggurat** dominated each city. Most people lived in one-story houses with rooms arranged around a small courtyard.

> **Underline the sentence that describes the kind of houses in which most Sumerians lived.**

Sumerian art is renowned for sculpture and jewelry. Sculptors created statues of gods for the temples, and made small objects of ivory or rare woods. Jewelers worked with imported gold, silver, and fine stones. Earrings and other items found in the region show that Sumerian jewelers knew advanced methods for putting gold pieces together.

The Sumerians also developed a special art form called the cylinder seal. The cylinder seal was a small stone cylinder that was engraved with designs and could be rolled over wet clay to decorate containers or to "sign" documents.

Music played an important role in Sumerian society. Musicians played stringed instruments, reed pipes, drums, and tambourines both for entertainment and for special occasions.

> **Name four types of musical instruments played by Sumerians.**
> _____
> _____
> _____
> _____

CHALLENGE ACTIVITY

Critical Thinking: Drawing Inferences Consider the invention of writing and of the wheel. As you go through a normal day keep a list of the things you do that rely on one or the other of these two inventions.

Mesopotamia and the Fertile Crescent

Section 4

MAIN IDEAS

1. The Babylonians conquered Mesopotamia and created a code of law.
2. Later invasions of Mesopotamia changed the region's culture.
3. The Phoenicians built a trading society in the eastern Mediterranean region.

Key Terms and People

monarch a ruler of a kingdom or empire

Hammurabi's Code the earliest known written collection of laws, comprising 282 laws
  that dealt with almost every part of life

chariot a wheeled, horse-drawn battle car

Nebuchadnezzar the Chaldean king who rebuilt Babylon

alphabet a set of letters than can be combined to form written words

Section Summary

THE BABYLONIANS CONQUER MESOPOTAMIA

By 1800 BC, a powerful city-state had arisen in
Babylon, an old Sumerian city on the Euphrates.
Babylon's greatest **monarch** (MAH-nark),
Hammurabi, conquered all of Mespotamia.

During his 42-year reign, Hammurabi oversaw
many building and irrigation projects, improved
the tax collection system, and brought prosperity
through increased trade. He is most famous, however,
for **Hammurabi's Code**, the earliest known written
collection of laws. It contained laws on everything
from trade, loans, and theft to injury, marriage, and
murder. Some of its ideas are still found in laws today.
The code was important not only for how thorough it
was, but also because it was written down for all to see.

> On what river was the city of
> Babylon located?
> _____
> _____

> Why do you think it is important
> for laws to be written down?
> _____
> _____
> _____

INVASIONS OF MESOPOTAMIA

Several other civilizations developed in and around
the Fertile Crescent. As their armies battled each

Section 4, continued

other for Mesopotamia's fertile land, control of the region passed from one empire to another. The Hittites of Asia Minor captured Babylon in 1595 BC with strong iron weapons and the skillful use of the **chariot** on the battlefield. After the Hittite king was killed, the Kassites captured Babylon and ruled for almost 400 years.

The Assyrians were the next group to conquer all of Mesopotamia. They ruled from Nineveh, a city in the north. The Assyrians collected taxes, enforced laws, and raised troops through local leaders. The Assyrians also built roads to link distant parts of the empire. In 612 BC the Chaldeans, a group from the Syrian Desert, conquered the Assyrians.

Nebuchadnezzar (neb-uh-kuhd-NEZ-uhr), the most famous Chaldean king, rebuilt Babylon into a beautiful city. According to legend, his grand palace featured the famous Hanging Gardens. The Chaldeans revived Sumerian culture and made notable advances in astronomy and mathematics.

> **Name four groups that conquered all of Mesopotamia after the Babylonians.**
> _____
> _____
> _____
> _____

> **Which older Mesopotamian civilization did the Chaldeans admire and study?**
> _____
> _____

THE PHOENICIANS

Phoenicia, at the western end of the Fertile Crescent along the Mediterranean Sea, created a wealthy trading society. Fleets of fast Phoenician trading ships sailed throughout the Mediterranean and even into the Atlantic Ocean, building trade networks and founding new cities. The Phoenicians' most lasting achievement, however, was the **alphabet**, a major development that has had a huge impact on the ancient world and on our own.

> **On what body of water were most Phoenician colonies located?**
> _____
> _____

CHALLENGE ACTIVITY

Critical Thinking: Drawing Inferences Make a timeline with approximate dates showing the various empires and invasions that characterized the history of Mesopotamia up to the time of the Chaldeans.

Interactive Reader and Study Guide

Ancient Egypt and Kush

CHAPTER SUMMARY

Egypt	Kush
Women worked in the home	Women worked in _____
Led by pharaohs (male)	Led by _____
Worshipped _____, with a human head and man's body	Worshipped lion-headed god _____
Developed pictograph writing style called _____	Developed pictograph writing style called Meroitic
Built _____ pyramids to bury dead kings	Built _____ pyramids to bury dead kings

COMPREHENSION AND CRITICAL THINKING

Use the answers to the following questions to fill in the graphic organizer above.

1. Explain What were three similarities between the Kush and Egyptian cultures?

_____

_____

2. Identify Cause and Effect How was the position of women in Kush society different than that of Egyptian women?

_____

_____

3. Evaluate Why do you think houses in Egypt were different than houses in Kush?

_____

_____

4. Draw a Conclusion How were the two cultures similar? How were the two cultures distinctly different?

_____

_____

Ancient Egypt and Kush

MAIN IDEAS

1. Egypt was called the "gift of the Nile" because the Nile River gave life to the desert.
2. Civilization developed along the Nile in this region after people began farming.
3. Strong kings unified all of Egypt.

Key Terms and People

cataract steep river rapids, almost impossible to sail by boat

delta a triangle-shaped area of land made of soil deposited by a river

Menes an Egyptian leader who united both upper and lower Egypt into one kingdom

pharaoh ruler of unified Egypt, literally means "great house"

dynasty a series of rulers from the same family

Section Summary

THE GIFT OF THE NILE

The existence of Egypt was based solely around the Nile, the world's longest river. The Nile carries water from central Africa through a vast stretch of desert land. The Nile also carries fine black silt as it flows. When the river floods, it deposits this soil along its banks. The land surrounding the Nile Valley was arid desert, so the area along the river was the lifeline for everyone who lived in the region. The river was so important to people that Egypt was called the "gift of the Nile."

Ancient Egypt developed along a 750-mile stretch of the Nile, and was originally organized into two kingdoms—Upper Egypt and Lower Egypt. Upper Egypt was located upriver in relation to the Nile's flow. Lower Egypt was the northern region and was located downriver.

Cataracts, or steep rapids, marked the southern border of Upper Egypt. Lower Egypt was centered in the river **delta**, a triangle-shaped area of land

> **What gifts did the Nile give to the land along its banks?**
> _____
> _____
> _____

> **How could a cataract serve as a natural protective barrier?**
> _____
> _____
> _____

made of soil deposited by the river. In midsummer the Nile would flood Upper Egypt. In the fall the river would flood Lower Egypt.

CIVILIZATION DEVELOPS ALONG THE NILE

With dry desert all around, it is no wonder that ancient settlers were attracted to this abundant and protected area of fertile farmland. Hunter-gatherers first moved to the area around 12,000 years ago and found plenty of meat and fish to hunt and eat. By 4500 BC farmers were living in villages and growing wheat and barley. They were also raising cattle and sheep.

Around 3200 BC the Egyptian villages became organized into two kingdoms. The capital of Lower Egypt was located in the northwest Nile Delta at a town called Pe. The capital city of Upper Egypt was called Nekhen. It was located on the west bank of the Nile.

> Why would hunter-gatherers be attracted to the banks of a river that floods every year?
> _____
> _____
> _____
> _____

> Why do you think Egyptian farming villages banded together and became kingdoms?
> _____
> _____
> _____
> _____

KINGS UNIFY EGYPT

Around 3100 BC **Menes** (MEE-neez), the king of Upper Egypt, invaded Lower Egypt. He married a princess there in order to unite the two kingdoms under his rule. Menes was the first **pharaoh**, which literally means ruler of a "great house." He also started the first Egyptian **dynasty**, or series of rulers from the same family. He built a new capital city, Memphis, which became a popular cultural center. His dynasty ruled for nearly 200 years.

CHALLENGE ACTIVITY

Critical Thinking: Drawing Inferences Villages developed when people stopped being hunter-gatherers and start growing their food. Some people in villages became powerful leaders who united several villages and their people into larger territories under one organization. Imagine that you are a village leader in ancient Egypt and that you are interested in uniting several villages. Write a speech explaining why you want to unite the villages and why people should agree with you.

Ancient Egypt and Kush

> **MAIN IDEAS**
> 1. In early Egyptian society, pharaohs ruled as gods and were at the top of the social structure.
> 2. Religion shaped Egyptian life.
> 3. The pyramids of Egypt were built as tombs for the pharaohs.

Key Terms and People

Old Kingdom the third Egyptian dynasty, which lasted nearly 500 years

Khufu the most famous pharaoh of the Old Kingdom

nobles people from rich and powerful families

afterlife life after death, a widely held ancient Egyptian belief

mummies the Egyptian method of preserving dead bodies by wrapping them in cloth

elite people of wealth and power

pyramids huge stone tombs with four triangle-shaped walls that meet at a top point

engineering the application of scientific knowledge for practical purposes

Academic Vocabulary

acquire to get

method a way of doing something

Section Summary

EARLY EGYPTIAN SOCIETY

Around 2700 BC the third dynasty, or **Old Kingdom**, came to power in Egypt. During the next 500 years, the Egyptians developed a political system based on the belief that the pharaoh was both a king and a god. The most famous pharaoh of the Old Kingdom was **Khufu**, in whose honor the largest of the pyramids was built.

Although the pharaoh owned everything, he was also held personally responsible if anything went wrong. He was expected to make trade profitable. It was up to him to prevent war. To manage these duties, he appointed government officials, mostly

> Would you say that there was any distinction between religion and politics in Egypt's Old Kingdom? Why or why not?
>
> _____
> _____
> _____
> _____

from his family. Social classes developed, with
the pharaoh at the top and **nobles** from rich and
powerful families making up the upper class. The
middle class included some government officials,
the scribes, and rich craftspeople. Most people,
including farmers, belonged to the lower class. The
pharaoh often used people from the lower class as a
source of labor.

> Of the upper, middle, and lower classes, which was the largest in ancient Egypt?
> _____
> _____

During the time of the Old Kingdom, trade
between Egypt and other areas developed. Traders
sailed the Mediterranean Sea, south on the Nile
River, and on the Red Sea to **acquire** gold, copper,
ivory, slaves, wood, incense, and myrrh.

RELIGION AND EGYPTIAN LIFE

The Old Kingdom formalized a religious structure
that everyone was expected to follow. Over time
certain cities built temples and were associated
with particular gods.

Much of Egyptian religion focused on the
afterlife. Each person's *ka* (KAH), or life force,
existed after death but remained linked to the
body. To keep the *ka* from suffering, the Egyptians
developed a **method** called embalming to preserve
bodies. The bodies were preserved as **mummies**,
specially treated bodies wrapped in cloth. Only
royalty and other members of the **elite** could afford
to have mummies made.

> What is the *ka*?
> _____
> _____

THE PYRAMIDS

Pyramids, spectacular stone monuments, were
built to house dead rulers. Many pyramids are still
standing today, amazing reminders of Egyptian
engineering.

> Why do you think the Egyptians believed that royal burial sites were so important?
> _____
> _____
> _____
> _____

CHALLENGE ACTIVITY

Critical Thinking: Drawing Inferences Is the way the ancient Egyptians
viewed the pharaoh different or the same as the way we view the U.S.
president? Write a one-page essay considering whether a god-king
pharaoh ruling today would be loved or hated by his people.

Ancient Egypt and Kush

MAIN IDEAS

1. The Middle Kingdom was a period of stable government between periods of disorder.
2. In the New Kingdom, Egyptian trade and military power reached their peak, but Egypt's greatness did not last.
3. Work and daily life were different among Egypt's social classes.

Key Terms and People

Middle Kingdom period of stability and order in ancient Egypt between about 2050 and 1750 BC

New Kingdom the height of Egypt's power and glory, between 1550 and 1050 BC

trade routes paths followed by traders

Queen Hatshepsut New Kingdom ruler renowned for expanding Egyptian trade

Ramses the Great important New Kingdom pharaoh who defended Egypt from invaders and strengthened defenses

Academic Vocabulary

contracts binding legal agreements

Section Summary

THE MIDDLE KINGDOM

The Old Kingdom ended with the pharaohs in debt. Ambitious nobles serving in government positions managed to take power from the pharaohs and rule Egypt for nearly 160 years. Finally, a powerful pharaoh regained control of Egypt around 2050 BC and started a peaceful period of rule. This era was called the **Middle Kingdom** and lasted until Southwest Asian invaders conquered Lower Egypt around 1750 BC.

> From where did the raiders who ended the Middle Kingdom come?
>
> _____
>
> _____

THE NEW KINGDOM

When an Egyptian named Ahmose (AHM-ohs) drove away the invaders and declared himself king of Egypt in 1550 BC, he ushered in Egypt's eighteenth dynasty and the start of the **New Kingdom**.

Responding to invasions, Egypt took control of the invasion routes and became the leading military power in the region. Egypt's empire extended from the Euphrates River in the northeast to Nubia in the south. These conquests made Egypt rich through gifts and vastly expanded **trade routes**. One of Egypt's rulers in particular, **Queen Hatshepshut**, was active in establishing new paths for traders.

> Which direction would you go from Egypt to reach Nubia?
>
> _____
>
> _____

Despite the strong leadership of **Ramses the Great**, a tide of invasions from Southwest Asia and from the west eventually reduced Egypt to violence and disorder.

WORK AND DAILY LIFE

During the Middle and New Kingdoms, Egypt's population continued to grow and became more complex. Professional and skilled workers like scribes, artisans, artists, and architects were honored. These roles in society were usually passed on in families, with young boys learning a trade from their father.

> Which professional workers probably designed the pyramids?
>
> _____
>
> _____

For farmers and peasants, who made up the vast majority of the population, life never changed. In addition to hard work on the land, they were required to pay taxes and were subject to special labor duty at any time. Only slaves were beneath them in social status.

> For farmers, did daily life in Egypt change much with the rise and fall of dynasties and kingdoms?
>
> _____
>
> _____

Most Egyptian families lived in their own homes. Boys were expected to marry young and start their own families. Women worked in the home, but many also had jobs outside the home. Egyptian women had the legal rights to own property, make **contracts**, and divorce their husbands.

CHALLENGE ACTIVITY

Critical Thinking: Drawing Inferences In a structured society, such as the Middle Kingdom in ancient Egypt, what are the advantages and disadvantages of young people learning a trade from their fathers? Write a brief essay explaining your answer.

Ancient Egypt and Kush

Section 4

> **MAIN IDEAS**
> 1. The Egyptians developed a writing system using hieroglyphics.
> 2. The Egyptians created magnificent temples, tombs, and works of art.

Key Terms and People

hieroglyphics Egyptian writing system, one of the world's first, which used symbols

papyrus long-lasting, paper-like substance made from reeds

Rosetta Stone a stone slab discovered in 1799 that was inscribed with hieroglyphics and their Greek meanings

sphinxes huge ancient Egyptian statues of imaginary creatures with the heads of people and bodies of lions

obelisk a tall, four-sided pillar that is pointed on top

King Tutankhamen a pharaoh whose tomb was untouched by raiders, leaving much information about Egyptian art and burial practices

Section Summary

EGYPTIAN WRITING

Egyptians invented one of the world's first writing systems, using a series of images, symbols, and pictures called **hieroglyphics** (hy-ruh-GLIH-fiks). Each symbol represented one or more sounds in the Egyptian language.

At first hieroglyphics were carved in stone. Later they were written with brushes and ink on **papyrus** (puh-PY-ruhs). Because papyrus didn't decay, many ancient Egyptian texts still survive, including government records, historical records, science texts, medical manuals, and literary works such as *The Book of the Dead*. The discovery of the **Rosetta Stone** in 1799 provided the key to reading Egyptian writing. The Rosetta Stone contained the same text inscribed in both hieroglyphics and Greek.

> What language helped scholars to understand the meaning of hieroglyphics on the Rosetta Stone?
>
> _____
>
> _____

EGYPT'S GREAT TEMPLES

Egyptian architects are known not only for the pyramids but also for their magnificent temples.

Section 4, *continued*

The temples were lavishly designed with numerous statues and beautifully painted walls and pillars. **Sphinxes** and **obelisks** were usually found near the entrances to the temples.

> Besides architects, what two groups of skilled artists worked to decorate Egyptian temples?
>
> _____
> _____
> _____

EGYPTIAN ART

Ancient Egyptians were masterful artists and many of their greatest works are found in either the temples or the tombs of the pharaohs. Most Egyptians, however, never saw these paintings because only kings, priests, or other important people could enter these places.

> Who got to see ancient Egyptian sculpture and painting?
>
> _____
> _____
> _____

Egyptian paintings depict a variety of subjects, from crowning kings to illustrating religious rituals and showing scenes from daily life. The paintings also have a particular style, with people drawn as if they were twisting as they walked, and in different sizes depending upon their stature in society. In contrast, animals appear more realistically. The Egyptians were also skilled stone and metal workers, creating beautiful statues and jewelry.

Much of what we know about Egyptian art and burial practices comes from the tomb of **King Tutankhamen**, one of the few Egyptian tombs that was left untouched by raiders looking for valuables. The tomb was discovered in 1922.

> Why is King Tutankhamen's tomb so important for the study of Egyptian history?
>
> _____
> _____
> _____
> _____

CHALLENGE ACTIVITY

Critical Thinking: Analyzing Using the library or an online resource, find a key to translate Egyptian hieroglyphics into English. Write a message using hieroglyphics. Trade your message with another student to see if you can read each other's messages. Be sure to provide a copy of your message and the translation to your teacher. Do you prefer to write in hieroglyphics or English? Write a paragraph explaining your preference.

Interactive Reader and Study Guide

Ancient Egypt and Kush

MAIN IDEAS
1. The geography of early Nubia helped civilization develop there.
2. Kush and Egypt traded but they also fought.
3. Later Kush became a trading power with a unique culture.
4. Both internal and external conflicts lead to the decline of Kush.

Key Terms and People

Piankhi Kushite king who conquered all of Egypt

trade network a system of people in different lands who trade goods back and forth

merchants traders

exports items sent for sale in other countries or regions

imports goods brought in from other countries or regions

Queen Shanakhdakheto the first woman to rule Kush

King Ezana Aksumite king who destroyed Meroë and took over the kingdom of Kush

Academic Vocabulary

authority power or influence

Section Summary

THE GEOGRAPHY OF EARLY NUBIA

The kingdom of Kush developed in Nubia, south of Egypt. Just as in Egypt, yearly Nile floods provided fertile soil and farming thrived. The area was also rich in gold, copper, and stone. Kerma (KAR-muh), the capital city on the Nile, was protected by a cataract, or stretch of shallow rapids. As time passed Kushite society became more complex.

> What valuable resources were important to Kush's prosperity?
> _____
> _____
> _____
> _____

KUSH AND EGYPT

Kush and Egypt were trading partners. The Kushite sent slaves to Egypt. They also sent gold, copper, ebony, and ivory. At times Kush and Egypt were at war. Around 1500 BC, Thutmose I invaded Kush and left the palace at Kerma in ruins. Kush became

Name _____ Class _____ Date _____

Section 5, *continued*

free from Egypt in about 1050 BC. By around
850 BC Kush was a power again. During the 700s,
under the king Kashta, the Kushites began to invade
Egypt. Kashta's son, **Piankhi** (PYANG-kee),
conquered all of Egypt by the time he died in 716
BC. Piankhi's brother, Shabaka (SHAB-uh-kuh),
became pharaoh of the twenty-fifth, or Kushite,
dynasty. Egyptian culture thrived. But by 670 BC,
Assyrians invaded Egypt. Their iron weapons were
better than the bronze weapons of Kush. Over time,
the Assyrians pushed the Kushites back to Nubia.

> For about how many years was Kush under Egyptian control?
> _____
> _____

LATER KUSH

After Kush lost control of Egypt, it developed trade
to make itself rich again. Meroë (MER-oh-wee)
became the center of a **trade network**. Africa's first
iron industry developed here because iron ore and
wood for fuel were available. The Kushites sent
goods to Egypt. From there, Egyptian and Greek
merchants shipped goods to the Mediterranean
and beyond. Kush's **exports** included gold, pottery,
iron tools, ivory, leopard skins, and slaves. **Imports**
included luxury items from Egypt, Asia, and the
Mediterranean.

> What industry helped make Kush a rich and successful kingdom again?
> _____
> _____

The Kushites worshipped their own gods and
developed their own writing. Women were active
in society, and some rose to positions of **authority**.
Queen Shanakhdakheto (shah-nahk-dah-KEE-toh)
was the first of many women who ruled Kush.

> How was the position of women in Kushite society different than that of women in most other ancient civilizations?
> _____
> _____
> _____
> _____

THE DECLINE OF KUSH

By the AD 300s, another trading center, Aksum
(AHK-soom), located in what is now Eritrea, began
competing with Kush. Soon trade routes bypassed
Meroë, weakening Kush. The Aksum leader **King
Ezana** (AY-zah-nah) invaded, and Kush fell.

> Circle the name and kingdom of the ruler who eventually defeated Kush.

CHALLENGE ACTIVITY

Critical Thinking: Solving Problems Pretend you are a Kushite leader in
850 BC. Write a short essay explaining your plan to defeat Egypt.

Interactive Reader and Study Guide

Ancient India

CHAPTER SUMMARY

Aryan invasion of Indus and Ganges	led to	development of the caste system
unification of India into empires	led to	stability and prosperity
development of religion	led to	changes in roles of early Indian kings
stability of early Indian empires	led to	advances in arts and sciences

COMPREHENSION AND CRITICAL THINKING

Use information from the graphic organizer to answer the following questions.

1. Recall Which group introduced and developed the caste system in India?

_____

_____

2. Identify Cause and Effect Why does the unification of civilizations usually lead to prosperity and stability?

_____

_____

3. Evaluate Why do you think religion played such an important role in the way rulers were regarded in early civilizations?

_____

_____

4. Draw a Conclusion What characteristic of a civilization usually provides a sound basis for advances in arts and sciences?

_____

_____

Ancient India

> **MAIN IDEAS**
> 1. The geography of India includes high mountains, great rivers and heavy seasonal rain.
> 2. Harappan civilization developed along the Indus River.
> 3. The Aryan invasion of India changed the region's civilization.

Key Terms and People

subcontinent a large landmass smaller than a continent

monsoon seasonal wind patterns that cause wet and dry seasons

Sanskrit ancient India's most influential language

Section Summary

GEOGRAPHY OF INDIA

India is home to one of the world's earliest civilizations. India is so huge it's called a **subcontinent**, which is a large landmass that is smaller than a continent. A subcontinent is usually separated from a continent by physical features, such as mountains. The world's highest mountains, the Himalayas, are in India. India also has a vast desert, many fertile plains, and rugged plateaus. The Indus River, which flows from the Himalayas and is located mainly in present-day Pakistan, is the cradle of ancient Indian civilization. As in Egypt and Kush, the flooding river created fertile plains where people first settled. India's hot and humid climate is heavily influenced by **monsoons**, wind patterns that cause wet and dry seasons.

> Circle the name of the world's highest mountains.

> What two natural cycles affected agricultural development in the Indus valley?
> _____
> _____
> _____

HARAPPAN CIVILIZATION

India's first civilization was the Harappan civilization, which developed along the Indus River

Interactive Reader and Study Guide

valley. Named after the ancient city of Harappa, archaeologists believe Harappans thrived between 2300 and 1700 BC. In fact, most information about Harappans comes from the ruins of Harappa and another major city, Mohenjo Daro. Each city was well planned and built in the shadow of a fortress that could easily oversee the city streets.

The cities were very advanced. Most houses had indoor plumbing. The Harappans developed beautiful artisan crafts and a system of weights and measures. They also developed India's first writing system, but scholars have not been able to read it. Because of this, we know little for sure about the Harappan government, though it is thought that there were kings, who might have been thought of as gods. It's also unclear why the Harappan civilization crumbled.

Why was it an advantage for the streets of Mohenjo Daro and Harappa to be viewed from a fortress?

_____
_____
_____
_____

Why do you think we know so little about the Harappans?

_____
_____
_____

ARYAN INVASION

Originally nomads from Central Asia, the Aryans had taken over the Indus and Ganges River valleys by 1200 BC. Unlike the Harappans, they had no central government and they did not build planned cities. Aryans lived in small communities run by a local leader, or raja. Aryan groups fought each other as often as they fought outsiders.

The Aryans spoke **Sanskrit** and developed a rich tradition of poems and hymns that survived from generation to generation by word of mouth. People later figured out how to write in Sanskrit. The huge lasting influence of these early written works made Sanskrit the most important language of ancient India. Much of what we know about the early Aryans comes to us through Sanskrit records.

The early Aryans had a rich and expressive language, but they did not write. How did they preserve their poems and their history without writing?

_____
_____
_____
_____

CHALLENGE ACTIVITY

Critical Thinking: Drawing Inferences Write a short essay explaining what you think might have happened to the Harappan civilization.

Ancient India

Section 2

MAIN IDEAS

1. Indian society divided into distinct social classes under the Aryans.
2. The Aryans practiced a religion known as Brahmanism.
3. Hinduism developed out of Brahmanism and influences from other cultures.
4. The Jains reacted to Hinduism by breaking away to form their own religion.

Key Terms and People

caste system a division of Indian society into groups based on a person's birth, wealth, or occupation

Hinduism the most widespread religion in India today

reincarnation the belief that the soul, once a person dies, is reborn in another person

karma the effects that good or bad actions have on a person's soul

Jainism a nonviolent religion based on the teachings of Mahavira

nonviolence the avoidance of violent actions

Section Summary

INDIAN SOCIETY DIVIDES

Aryan society was divided into social classes. There were four main groups, called *varnas*. The Brahmins (BRAH-muhns) were priests and were the highest ranking varna. The Kshatriyas (KSHA-tree-uhs) were rulers or warriors. The Vaisyas (VYSH-yuhs) were commoners, including farmers, craftspeople, and traders. The Sudras (SOO-drahs) were laborers and servants.

This **caste system** became more complex, dividing Indian society into groups based on rank, wealth or occupation. Castes were family based. If you were born into a caste, you would probably stay in it for your whole life. Life for the lower castes was difficult, but those who had no caste, called untouchables, were ostracized.

> Rank the main groups of the Aryan social classes in order of importance, with one (1) being highest and four (4) being the lowest:
> Brahmins
> Sudras
> Kshatriyas
> Vaisyas

> In ancient India, why was it important to belong to some caste?
> _____
> _____
> _____

BRAHMANISM

The religion practiced by the Brahmins became known as Brahmanism. Brahmanism was perhaps the most important part of ancient Indian life, as shown by the high status of the priest caste. The religion was based on the four Vedas, writings that contained ancient sacred hymns and poems. Over time, Aryan Brahmins and scholars wrote their thoughts about the Vedas. These thoughts were compiled into Vedic texts. The texts described rituals, explained how to perform sacrifices, and offered reflections from religious scholars.

> The Vedas existed before Sanskrit was written down. At first, how had they been preserved?
>
> _____
> _____
> _____

HINDUISM DEVELOPS

Hinduism is India's largest religion today. It developed from Brahmanism and other influences. Hindus believe that there are many gods, but all gods are part of a universal spirit called Brahmin. Hindus believe everyone has a soul, or atman, and the soul longs to join with Brahmin. This happens when the soul recognizes that the world we live in is an illusion. Hindus believe this understanding takes several lifetimes, so **reincarnation**, or rebirth, is necessary. How you are reborn depends upon your **karma**, or your actions in life. In the caste system, those who have good karma are born to higher castes. Those with bad karma are born into lower castes or maybe even an animal.

> What is the Hindu name for the soul?
>
> _____
> _____

> Think about why you believe that the real world actually exists. Do you think you can prove that it does? Answer yes or no.
>
> _____
> _____

The religion of **Jainism** developed in reaction to Hinduism. Jainism is based upon the principle of **nonviolence**, or ahimsa.

CHALLENGE ACTIVITY

Critical Thinking: Drawing Inferences Do ahimsa, reincarnation, or karma have any relevance in our society? Pick one or more of these terms and write a one-page essay on how such terms could, or could not, be used in your world.

Ancient India

MAIN IDEAS

1. Siddhartha Gautama searched for wisdom in many ways.

2. The teachings of Buddhism deal with finding peace.

3. Buddhism spread far from where it began in India.

Key Terms and People

fasting going without food

meditation focusing the mind on spiritual ideas

the Buddha the "Enlightened One"

Buddhism religion based on the teachings of the Buddha

nirvana a state of perfect peace

missionaries people who spread and teach religious beliefs

Section Summary

SIDDARTHA'S SEARCH FOR WISDOM

Not everyone in India accepted Hinduism. In the late 500s BC, a major new religion began to develop from questions posed by a young prince named Siddhartha Gautama (si-DAHR-tuh GAU-tuh-muh). Siddhartha was born to a wealthy family and led a life of comfort, but he wondered at the pain and suffering he saw all around him. By the age of 30, Siddharta left his home and family to travel India. He talked to many priests and wise men, but he was not satisfied with their answers.

Siddhartha did not give up. He wandered for years through the forests trying to free himself from daily concerns by **fasting** and **meditating**. After six years, Siddhartha sat down under a tree and meditated for seven weeks. He came up with an answer to what causes human suffering. Suffering is caused by wanting what one does not have, wanting

> **Why did Prince Siddhartha leave a comfortable home and loving family?**
>
> _____
> _____
> _____
> _____

> **Can you think of a form of human suffering not covered by one of Siddhartha's three categories? If so, state briefly what it is.**
>
> _____
> _____
> _____
> _____

Section 3, *continued*

to keep what one likes and already has, and not wanting what one dislikes but has. He began to travel and teach his ideas, and was soon called **the Buddha**, or "Enlightened One." From his teachings sprang the religion **Buddhism**.

TEACHINGS OF BUDDHISM

Buddhism is intent on relieving human suffering. It is based upon the Four Noble Truths. These truths are: Suffering and unhappiness are part of life; suffering stems from our desire for pleasure and material goods; people can overcome their desires and reach **nirvana**, a state of perfect peace, which ends the cycle of reincarnation; and people can follow an eightfold path to nirvana, overcoming desire and ignorance.

> **What is the name of the central teachings of Buddhism?**
>
> _____
>
> _____

These teachings were similar to some Hindu concepts, but went against some traditional Hindu ideas. Buddhism questioned the need for animal sacrifice. It also challenged the authority of the Brahmins. The Buddah said that each individual could reach salvation on his or her own. Buddhism also opposed the caste system.

> **Buddhist texts often refer to "the compassionate Buddha." Why is this term appropriate?**
>
> _____
>
> _____
>
> _____

BUDDHISM SPREADS

Buddhism spread quickly throughout India. With the help of Indian king Asoka, Buddhist **missionaries** were sent to other countries to teach their religious beliefs. Buddhism quickly took hold in neighboring countries like Nepal, Sri Lanka, and China. Buddhism soon became very influential in Japan and Korea. In modern times, Buddhism has become a major global religion.

> **Name one way in which Buddhist doctrine is similar to democracy.**
>
> _____
>
> _____
>
> _____

CHALLENGE ACTIVITY

Critical Thinking: Drawing Inferences Could you leave your family, home, and everything you know to preach what you believe to be a spiritual truth? You are preparing to follow the Buddha. Write a goodbye letter to your family explaining why you have chosen this life of sacrifice.

> **MAIN IDEAS**
> 1. The Mauryan Empire unified most of India.
> 2. Gupta rulers promoted Hinduism within their empires.

Key Terms and People

Candragupta Maurya Indian military leader who first unified India and founded the Mauryan Empire

Asoka Candragupta's grandson and last ruler of the Mauryan Empire

Candra Gupta II ruler who brought great prosperity and stability to India

Academic Vocabulary

establish to set up or create

Section Summary

MAURYAN EMPIRE UNIFIES INDIA

Under Aryan rule, India was divided into several states with no central leader. Then, during the 300s BC, the conquests of Alexander the Great brought much of India into his empire. An Indian military leader named **Candragupta Maurya** followed Alexander's example and seized control of the entire northern part of India. The Mauryan Empire lasted for 150 years.

Candragupta's complex government included a huge army and a network of spies. He taxed the population heavily for the protection he offered. Eventually, Candragupta became a Jainist monk and gave up his throne to his son. His family continued to expand the Indian empire.

Candragupta's grandson, **Asoka**, was the strongest ruler of the Mauryan dynasty. The empire thrived under his rule. But at last, tired of killing and war, Asoka converted to Buddhism. He sent Buddhist missionaries to other countries and

> Who inspired Indian leader Candragupta Maurya to unify India for the first time?
> _____
> _____

> What is the relationship between Candragupta's government and the heavy taxes?
> _____
> _____
> _____
> _____
> _____

Section 4, *continued*

devoted the rest of his rule to improving the lives of his people. The rest of the family, however, did not follow Asoka's example. When Asoka died, his sons struggled for power and foreign invaders threatened the country. The Mauryan Empire fell in 184 BC India remained divided for about 500 years. The spread of Buddhism steadily increased, while Hinduism declined.

> Asoka is sometimes regarded as proof that national security can coexist with peace. Do you think a leader like Asoka could be effective in the world today? Why or why not?
> _____
> _____
> _____
> _____

GUPTA RULERS PROMOTE HINDUISM

A new dynasty was **established** in India. During the 300s AD, the Gupta Dynasty once again rose to unite and build the prosperity of India. Not only did the Guptas control India's military, they were devout Hindus and encouraged the revival of Hindu traditions and writings. The Guptas, however, also supported Jainism and Buddhism.

> Which dynasty ruled over a "golden age" of Indian civilization?
> _____
> _____

Indian civilization reached a high point under **Candra Gupta II** (not related to Candragupta Maurya). He poured money and resources into strengthening the country's borders, as well as promoting the arts, literature, and religion.

The Guptas believed the caste system supported stability. This was not good for women, whose role under the empire was very restricted. Women were expected to marry, in weddings arranged by their parents, and raise children. A woman had to obey her husband and had few rights.

> Name two flaws, from a democratic point of view, in Indian civilization under the Guptas.
> _____
> _____
> _____
> _____

The Gupta Dynasty lasted until fierce attacks by the Huns from Central Asia during the 400s drained the empire of its resources. India broke up once again into a patchwork of small states.

CHALLENGE ACTIVITY

Critical Thinking: Drawing Inferences Asoka was strongly influenced by Buddhism. Candra Gupta II followed Hinduism. Write an essay explaining which king you think was a better leader. How did their religion affect their rule? Keep in mind the situation of Indian society under both kings' reign.

Section 5

MAIN IDEAS

1. Indian artists created great works of religious art.
2. Sanskrit literature flourished during the Gupta period.
3. The Indians made scientific advances in metalworking, medicine and other sciences.

Key Terms and People

metallurgy the science of working with metals

alloy a mixture of two or more metals

Hindu-Arabic numerals the numbering system invented by Indian mathematicians and brought to Europe by Arabs; the numbers we use today

inoculation a method of injecting a person with a small dose of a virus to help him or her build up defenses to a disease

astronomy the study of stars and planets

Academic Vocabulary

process a series of steps by which a task is completed

Section Summary

RELIGIOUS ART

Both the Mauryan and Guptan empires unified India and created a stable environment where artists, writers, scholars, and scientists could thrive. Their works are still admired today. Much of the Indian art from this period was religious, inspired by both Hindu and Buddhist teachings. Many beautiful temples were built during this time and decorated with elaborate wood and stone carvings.

What was the main inspiration for art and literature during the Mauryan and Guptan empires?

_____

_____

SANSKRIT LITERATURE

Great works of literature were written in Sanskrit, the ancient Aryan language, during the Gupta

Sanskrit literature had a long tradition before it was written down. How were these early works first preserved?

_____

_____

Section 5, *continued*

Dynasty. The best-known works are the *Mahabharata* (muh-HAH-BAH-ruh-tuh) and the *Ramayana* (rah-MAH-yuh-nuh). The *Mahabharata*, a long story about the struggle between good and evil, is considered a classic Hindu text. The most famous passage is called the *Bhagavad Gita* (BUG-uh-vuhd-GEE-tah). The *Ramayana* is the story of the Prince Rama, a human incarnation of one of the three major Hindu gods, Vishnu, who fights demons and marries the beautiful princess Sita.

SCIENTIFIC ADVANCES

Scientific and scholarly work also blossomed during the early Indian empires. Most prominent was the development of **metallurgy**, the science of working with metals. Indian technicians and engineers made strong tools and weapons. They also invented **processes** for creating **alloys**. Alloys, such as steel or bronze, may be stronger or more useful than pure metals like iron or copper.

> **What major modern industry involves the production of a widely used alloy?**
>
> _____
>
> _____

The numbers we use today, called **Hindu-Arabic numerals**, were first developed by Indian mathematicians. They also created the concept of zero, upon which all modern math is based.

> **What mathematical concept expresses the idea of "none?"**
>
> _____
>
> _____

Other sciences also benefited from this period of Indian history. In medicine, Indians developed the technique of **inoculation**, which is injecting a person with a small dose of a virus to help him or her build up defenses to a disease. Doctors could even perform certain surgeries. India's fascination with **astronomy**, the study of stars and planets, led to the discovery of seven of the planets in our solar system.

> **Indians at this period did not have telescopes. How do you think they discovered planets?**
>
> _____
>
> _____
>
> _____
>
> _____

CHALLENGE ACTIVITY

Critical Thinking: Drawing Inferences Our modern society borrows significantly from the scientific and mathematical achievements of the early Indian empires. Write a short play, story, or essay describing how our modern world might look without these inventions.

Ancient China

CHAPTER SUMMARY

THE FIRST FIVE DYNASTIES

| XIA 2200 BC: According to legend, the first waterways were built | SHANG 1500 BC: Writing system begins | ZHOU 1100 BC: Social hierarchy, family structure, central authority | QIN 220 BC: Military regime, strong central government, harsh policies, roads, canals, Great Wall | HAN 200 BC: Poetry, central government preserved, paper, acupuncture, trade |

COMPREHENSION AND CRITICAL THINKING

Use information from the graphic organizer to answer the following questions.

1. Identify Which of the first five dynasties lasted the longest?

_____

_____

2. Draw Inferences Which dynasty improved on a rudimentary system of communication that had probably existed for 2000 years?

_____

_____

3. Evaluate Which dynasty kept some beneficial aspects of the former regime and ended its harsher aspects?

_____

_____

Ancient China

Section 1

MAIN IDEAS

1. China's physical geography made farming possible but travel and communication difficult.
2. Civilization began in China along the Huang He and Chang Jiang rivers.
3. China's first dynasties helped Chinese society develop and made many other achievements.

Key Terms and People

jade a hard gemstone

oracle a prediction

Section Summary

CHINA'S PHYSICAL GEOGRAPHY

China is a large country with many different geographical features. China is about the same size as the United States. Some geographical features separated groups of people within China, while other features separated China from the rest of the world. These features include the Gobi Desert, which spreads over much of China's north, and rugged mountains on the western frontier.

In which part of China is the Gobi Desert?

_____

_____

Low-lying plains in the east form one of the world's largest farming regions. Weather patterns vary widely across China. Two great rivers flow from west to east, the Huang He, or Yellow River, and the Chang Jiang, or Yangzi River.

CIVILIZATION BEGINS

Like other ancient peoples, people in China first settled along rivers. By 7000 BC farmers grew rice in the Chang Jiang Valley. Along the Huang He, they grew millet and wheat. Early Chinese also fished and hunted with bows and arrows. They raised

Where did the Chinese first grow rice?

_____

_____

Interactive Reader and Study Guide

pigs and sheep. Separate cultures developed along the two rivers. As populations grew, villages spread. A social order developed. The graves of the rich often contained objects made from **jade**.

CHINA'S FIRST DYNASTIES

Societies along the Huang He grew larger and more complex. Around 2200 BC, a legendary emperor called Yu the Great is said to have founded the Xia (SHAH) dynasty. It is believed that the first flood control channels were built during the Xia dynasty.

> **About how many years ago were the first flood control channels built in China?**
> _____
> _____

The first dynasty for which we have clear evidence is the Shang. It was firmly established by the 1500s BC. The Shang king and his family were at the top of the social order. Nobles and warrior leaders also had high rank. Artisans lived in groups depending on what they did for a living. Farmers worked hard but had little wealth. Taxes claimed much of what they earned. Slaves provided an important source of labor.

> **Which dynasty provided the basis for China's writing system?**
> _____
> _____

The Shang made many advances, including China's first writing system. The Chinese symbols that are used today are based on those of the Shang period. Priests carved questions about the future on cattle bones and turtle shells, which were then heated, causing them to crack. The priests believed they could "read" these cracks to predict the future. For this reason the bones were called **oracle** bones.

Artisans made beautiful bronze containers for cooking and religious ceremonies. They also made ornaments, knives, and axes from jade. The army developed war chariots and bronze body armor. Shang astrologers developed a calendar based on the cycles of the moon.

CHALLENGE ACTIVITY

Critical Thinking: Drawing Inferences Using the library or online resource, study ancient Chinese writing. Use some of these symbols to illustrate something you have learned about China.

Ancient China

┌───┐
MAIN IDEAS

1. The Zhou dynasty expanded China but then declined.

2. Confucius offered ideas to bring order to Chinese society.

3. Daoism and Legalism also gained followers.
└───┘

Key Terms and People

lords people of high rank

peasants farmers with small farms

Confucius most influential teacher in Chinese history

ethics moral values

Confucianism the ideas of Confucius

Daoism an early Chinese belief that stressed living in harmony with the universe

Laozi the most famous Daoist teacher

Legalism an early Chinese belief that people were bad by nature and needed to be controlled

Academic Vocabulary

structure the way something is set up or organized

Section Summary

THE ZHOU DYNASTY

The Zhou (JOH) came from the west and overthrew the Shang dynasty during the 1100s BC. Their armies defeated people in every direction. They expanded their rule south to the Chang Jiang river. The Zhou established a new political order. The king granted land to **lords** in return for loyalty and military assistance. Lords divided their land among lesser nobles. **Peasants** received a small plot of land and had to farm additional land for a noble. The social order brought by the Zhou lasted a long time, but the loyalty of the lords gradually lessened. They

┌─────────────────────────────────┐
How did the Zhou establish their
rule throughout China?

_____

_____
└─────────────────────────────────┘

began to fight each other. Family **structure**, which had been the foundation of Chinese life for centuries, was severely weakened. By the 400s BC, China had entered an era called the Warring States period.

CONFUCIUS AND SOCIETY

Toward the end of the Zhou period, a teacher named **Confucius** traveled through China. He taught that order in society stems from **ethics**, or moral values, and not laws. He wanted China to return to the ideas and practices from a time when people knew their proper roles in society. **Confucianism** has been a guiding force in human behavior and religious understanding in China and elsewhere through the centuries.

> Do you think that Confucius's ideas about virtue and kindness are strongly held in American society today? Why or why not?
>
> _____
> _____
> _____

DAOISM AND LEGALISM

Around the same time as Confucius, other influential beliefs arose in China. **Daoism** (DOW-ih-zum) stressed living in harmony with the Dao, the guiding force of all reality. Daoists believed that people should be like water and simply let things flow in a natural way. They regarded humans as just a part of nature, not superior to any other thing. **Laozi** was the most famous Daoist teacher.

> Underline the sentence that describes the way Daoists regard human life.

Legalism is different than both Daoism and Confucianism. Legalists believed that society needed strict laws to keep people in line. They believed in unity, efficiency, and punishment for bad conduct. They wanted the empire to continue to expand, so they urged the state to be always prepared for war. Legalists were the first to put their ideas into practice throughout China.

> Do you think that Legalism is strong force in American society today? Why or why not?
>
> _____
> _____
> _____

CHALLENGE ACTIVITY

Critical Thinking: Drawing Inferences Write a short play with two characters, a Daoist and a Legalist. Make sure each character clearly expresses his or her views on behavior, society, and government.

Interactive Reader and Study Guide

Ancient China

> **MAIN IDEAS**
> 1. The first Qin emperor created a strong but strict government.
> 2. A unified China was created through Qin policies and achievements.

Key Terms and People

Shi Huangdi literally "first emperor," the title the Qin king Ying Zheng gave himself

Great Wall a barrier built by the Qin that linked earlier walls across China's northern frontier

Section Summary

THE QIN EMPEROR'S STRONG GOVERNMENT

The Warring States period marked a time in China when several states battled each other for power. One state, the Qin (CHIN), built a strong army that defeated the armies of the other states. In 221 BC the Qin king Ying Zheng was able to unify China. He gave himself the title **Shi Huangdi** (SHEE hwahng-dee), which means "first emperor."

Shi Huangdi was a follower of Legalist beliefs. He created a strong government with strict laws and severe punishments. He ordered the burning of all books that did not agree with Legalism.

Shi Huangdi took land away from the lords. He divided China into 36 miltary districts. He made commoners work on goverment building projects.

> Do you think Shi Huangdi respected human or family values? Explain your answer.
> _____
> _____
> _____
> _____

A UNIFIED CHINA

Qin rule brought other major changes to China. Under Shi Huangdi, new policies and achievements united the Chinese people. The emperor set up a uniform system of law. Rules and punishments were to be the same in all parts of the empire. He also

> List three ways Shi Huangdi unified China.
> _____
> _____
> _____
> _____

standardized the written language. People everywhere were required to write using the same set of symbols. People from different regions could now communicate with each other in writing. This gave them a sense of shared culture and a common identity.

Shi Huangdi also set up a new monetary system. Standardized gold and copper coins became the currency for all of China. Weights and measures were also standardized. With all these changes and the unified writing system, trade became much easier. A new network of highways connected the capital to every part of the empire. Workers built canals to connect the country's rivers. Parts of the Qin irrigation system are still used today.

The completion of the **Great Wall** was a major Qin achievement. The Qin connected earlier pieces of the wall to form a long, unbroken structure that protected China from fierce northern nomads. Building the wall required years of labor from hundreds of thousands of soldiers and workers. Many of them died building the wall.

Although he unified China, many Chinese people hated Shi Huangdi's harsh ways. When he died in 210 BC, rebel forces formed across the country and tried to take over the government. After a period of disorder, the Qin palace was attacked and burned to the ground. Qin authority had disappeared. China fell into civil war.

> **Give three reasons why trade flourished under the Qin.**
> _____
> _____
> _____
> _____

> **What was the purpose of the Great Wall?**
> _____
> _____
> _____

CHALLENGE ACTIVITY

Critical Thinking: Drawing Inferences If a brutal dictator came to power in the United States, would you join a revolutionary group planning to overthrow the government? Be sure to consider the ideas of Confucianism and Daoism in your answer.

Ancient China

MAIN IDEAS
1. Han dynasty government was based on the ideas of Confucius.
2. Family life strengthened Han China.
3. The Han made many achievements in art, literature, and learning.

Key Terms and People

sundial a device that uses the position of shadows cast by the sun to tell time

seismograph a device that measures the strength of an earthquake

acupuncture the practice of inserting small needles through the skin at specific points to cure disease or relieve pain

Academic Vocabulary

innovation a new idea, method, or device

Section Summary

HAN DYNASTY GOVERNMENT

Liu Bang (lee-oo bang), a peasant, led the army that won control of China after the collapse of the Qin dynasty. He earned the people's loyalty and trust. He lowered taxes for farmers and made punishments less severe. He set up a government that built on the foundation begun by the Qin. Liu Bang's successor, Wudi (woo-dee), made Confucianism the official government policy of China. To get a government job, a person had to pass a test based on Confucian teachings. However, wealthy and influential families still controlled the government.

> Which feature of the Qin dynasty did the Han preserve?
> _____
> _____

FAMILY LIFE

A firm social order took hold during Han rule. In the Confucian view, peasants made up the second-highest class. Merchants occupied the lowest class because they merely bought and sold what others

> Why does Confucian thinking devalue merchants?
> _____
> _____
> _____

Interactive Reader and Study Guide

had made. However, this social division did not indicate wealth or power. Peasants were still poor and merchants were still rich.

During Wudi's reign, the family once again became the center of Chinese society. Children were taught from birth to respect their elders. Within the family, the father had absolute power. Han officials believed that if the family was strong and people obeyed the father, then people would obey the emperor, too. Chinese parents valued boys more highly than girls. Some women, however, still gained power. They could influence their sons' families. An older widow could even become the head of the family.

> **Who had absolute power in the family under the Han?**
> _____
> _____

> **Circle the sentence that explains which women could become heads of families.**

HAN ACHIEVEMENTS

The Han dynasty was a time of great accomplishments. Art and literature thrived, and inventors developed many useful devices. Han artists painted portraits and realistic scenes that showed everyday life. Poets developed new styles of verse. Historian Sima Qian wrote a complete history of China until the Han dynasty.

The Han Chinese invented paper. They made it by grinding plant fibers into a paste and then letting it dry in sheets. They made "books" by pasting sheets together into a long sheet that was rolled into a scroll.

Other Han **innovations** included the **sundial** and the **seismograph**. They developed the disinctive Chinese medical practice of **acupuncture** (AK-yoo-punk-cher). These and other Han inventions and advances are still used today.

> **Name the greatest and most far-reaching Han invention.**
> _____
> _____

CHALLENGE ACTIVITY

Critical Thinking: Drawing Inferences Could the Han dynasty have flourished so well if the Qin had not set up a strong government structure? Write a brief essay presenting your point of view on this question.

Section 5

MAIN IDEAS
1. Farming and manufacturing grew during the Han dynasty.
2. Trade routes linked China with the Middle East and Rome.
3. Buddhism came to China from India and gained many followers.

Key Terms and People

silk a soft, light, highly valued fabric made from the cocoons of silkworms

Silk Road a network of routes between China and the Mediterranean Sea

diffusion the spread of ideas from one culture to another

Academic Vocabulary

procedure the way a task is accomplished

Section Summary

FARMING AND MANUFACTURING

During the Han dynasty, many farming advances led to bigger harvests. Manufacturing methods improved. Master ironworkers developed the iron plow and the wheelbarrow, two devices that made farming vastly more efficient.

The centuries-old process of producing **silk** increased. Weavers used foot-powered looms to weave silk threads into beautiful fabric. Garments made from silk were very expensive. The Chinese were determined to keep their **procedure** for making silk a secret. Revealing this secret was punishable by death.

> Name two devices that made farming more efficient.
> _____
> _____
> _____

> Why do you think it was important to keep the silk production process a secret?
> _____
> _____
> _____

TRADE ROUTES

When Han armies conquered lands deep in Central Asia, they learned that people even farther west

Interactive Reader and Study Guide

wanted silk. Han leaders saw that they could make
a profit by bringing silk to Central Asia and trading
the cloth for strong, sturdy Central Asian horses.
The Central Asian people would take the silk to the
west and trade it for products they wanted.

> **Aside from Rome, where did many of the items traded for silk come from?**
> _____
> _____

Traders used a series of overland routes known
as the **Silk Road** to take Chinese goods to distant
buyers. Although traveling the Silk Road was
difficult and risky, it was worth it. Silk was so
popular in Rome, for example, that China grew
wealthy just from trading with the Romans. Traders
returned to China with gold, silver, precious stones,
and horses.

BUDDHISM COMES TO CHINA

Over time, the Han government became less stable.
Life became violent and uncertain. In this climate,
Buddhist missionaries from India began to attract
attention.

> **What did Buddhism provide that other beliefs lacked?**
> _____
> _____

Buddhism seemed to provide more hope than
the traditional Chinese beliefs did. At first, Indian
Buddhists had trouble explaining their religion to
the Chinese. Then they used the ideas of Daoism
to help describe Buddhist beliefs. Before long,
Buddhism caught on in China with both the rich
and poor.

> **Underline the sentence that describes how the Indian Buddhists made their religion understandable to the Chinese.**

Buddhism's introduction to China is an example
of **diffusion**, the spread of ideas from one culture
to another. Chinese culture adopted Buddhism and
changed in response to the new faith.

CHALLENGE ACTIVITY

Critical Thinking: Drawing Inferences Do you think it was difficult to
keep the origin of silk and its production process a secret? Write a brief
story about a woman who is dying to tell and her fear of the dire
consequences.

Interactive Reader and Study Guide

The Hebrews and Judaism

CHAPTER SUMMARY

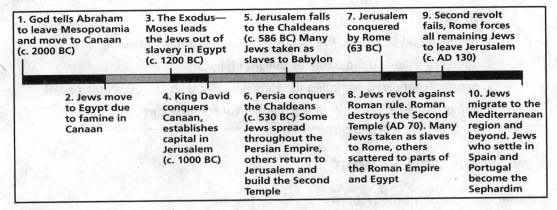

1. God tells Abraham to leave Mesopotamia and move to Canaan (c. 2000 BC)

2. Jews move to Egypt due to famine in Canaan

3. The Exodus—Moses leads the Jews out of slavery in Egypt (c. 1200 BC)

4. King David conquers Canaan, establishes capital in Jerusalem (c. 1000 BC)

5. Jerusalem falls to the Chaldeans (c. 586 BC) Many Jews taken as slaves to Babylon

6. Persia conquers the Chaldeans (c. 530 BC) Some Jews spread throughout the Persian Empire, others return to Jerusalem and build the Second Temple

7. Jerusalem conquered by Rome (63 BC)

8. Jews revolt against Roman rule. Roman destroys the Second Temple (AD 70). Many Jews taken as slaves to Rome, others scattered to parts of the Roman Empire and Egypt

9. Second revolt fails, Rome forces all remaining Jews to leave Jerusalem (c. AD 130)

10. Jews migrate to the Mediterranean region and beyond. Jews who settle in Spain and Portugal become the Sephardim

COMPREHENSION AND CRITICAL THINKING

Use information from the graphic organizer to answer the following questions.

1. Explain Who was the first Jew in the Bible? What did God ask of him?

_____

_____

2. Identify Cause and Effect Why did so many Jews leave Jerusalem in the first century AD?

_____

_____

_____

3. Evaluate How did the Diaspora affect Judaism?

_____

_____

4. Draw a Conclusion Which trip was the hardest one for Jews to make? Explain your answer.

_____

_____

_____

The Hebrews and Judaism

MAIN IDEAS

1. Abraham and Moses led the Hebrews to Canaan and to a new religion.
2. Strong kings united the Israelites to fight off invaders.
3. Invaders conquered and ruled the Hebrews after their kingdom broke apart.
4. Some women in Hebrew society made great contributions to their history.

Key Terms and People

Judaism the religion of the Hebrews

Abraham the biblical father of the Hebrew people

Moses Hebrew prophet who led the Jews from slavery in Egypt

Exodus the journey the Hebrews made from Egypt to Canaan, led by Moses

Ten Commandments moral code of laws that God handed down to Moses

David former outlaw who became king after the death of Saul, Israel's first king

Solomon David's son; became king of the Israelites

Diaspora the scattering of the Jews outside of Canaan

Section Summary

ABRAHAM AND MOSES LEAD THE HEBREWS

A people called the Hebrews (HEE-brooz) appeared in Southwest Asia sometime between 2000 and 1500 BC. Their writings describe the laws of their religion, **Judaism** (JOO-dee-i-zuhm). The Hebrew Bible, or Torah, traces the Hebrews back to a man named **Abraham**. The Bible says that God told Abraham to leave his home. God promised to lead him to a new land and to make his children into a mighty nation. Abraham moved to Canaan (KAY-nuhn). The Hebrews lived there for many years.

Some Hebrews later moved to Egypt. In time Egypt's ruler, the pharaoh, made them slaves. In the 1200s BC, God then told a man named **Moses** to demand the Hebrews' freedom. The pharaoh agreed only after a series of plagues struck Egypt.

> Circle the name of the people who appeared in Southwest Asia sometime between 2000 and 1500 BC.

> Underline the promise that God made to Abraham. Where did Abraham move?
>
> _____

Moses led the Hebrews out of Egypt in a journey called the **Exodus**. The Bible says that during this journey, God gave Moses two stone tablets with laws written on them, known as the **Ten Commandments**. The Hebrews were to worship only God and to value human life, self-control, and justice. The Hebrews reached Canaan after 40 years. They became the Israelites.

Why was Moses an important Hebrew leader?
_____
_____
_____
_____

KINGS UNITE THE ISRAELITES

A man named Saul fought the Philistines (FI-li-steenz) and became the first king of Israel. After Saul died a former outlaw named **David** became king. David was well-loved. He defeated the Philistines and other Jewish enemies. He captured the city of Jerusalem. It became Israel's new capital. David's son **Solomon** (SAHL-uh-muhn) became king next around 965 BC. Solomon was a strong king. He built a great temple in Jerusalem.

What three basic values are emphasized in the Ten Commandments?
_____
_____
_____
_____

Circle the names of the first three kings of Israel. Which king built a temple to God?
_____
_____

INVADERS CONQUER AND RULE

Soon after Solomon's death in 930 BC, Israel split into two kingdoms, Israel and Judah (JOO-duh). The people of Judah were known as Jews. Over the centuries the Jewish people were often conquered and enslaved. The scattering of the Jews outside of Canaan is known as the **Diaspora**. Jerusalem was conquered by the Greeks during the 330s BC. Judah regained independence for a time, but was conquered again in 63 BC, this time by the Romans.

WOMEN IN HEBREW SOCIETY

Men dominated Hebrew society, but some Hebrew women made great contributions to the culture.

CHALLENGE ACTIVITY

Critical Thinking: Drawing Inferences Write a set of ten commandments that reflects the responsibilities and rights of students and faculty for your school.

The Hebrews and Judaism

MAIN IDEAS

1. Beliefs in God, education, justice, and obedience anchor Jewish society.

2. Jewish beliefs are recorded in the Torah, the Hebrew Bible, and the Commentaries.

3. The Dead Sea Scrolls reveal many ancient Jewish beliefs.

4. The ideas of Judaism have helped shape later cultures.

Key Terms and People

monotheism belief in only one god

Torah the sacred text of Judaism

synagogue Jewish house of worship

prophets people said to receive messages from God to be taught to others

Talmud commentaries, stories, and folklore recorded to explain Jewish laws

Dead Sea Scrolls writings by Jews who lived about 2,000 years ago

Section Summary

JEWISH BELIEFS ANCHOR THEIR SOCIETY

Jewish society is founded upon religion. Judaism's main beliefs are beliefs in God, education, justice, and obedience.

Judaism is the oldest known religion to practice **monotheism**, the belief in only one god. The Jews call this god Yahweh (YAH-way). They believe that they are Yahweh's chosen people. The Jews say their history was guided through God's relationship with Abraham, Moses, and other leaders. Moral and religious laws, believed to be handed down from God, have guided Jewish society through their history and continue to do so today.

Besides the Ten Commandments, Jews believe that Moses recorded a whole set of laws governing Jewish behavior. These laws are called Mosaic law. These laws set down rules for everything including what to eat, when to work, and how to pray. Today

> Underline the four core values of Judaism.

> What is monotheism?
>
> _____
> _____
> _____

Section 2, *continued*

Orthodox Jews continue to follow all of the Mosaic laws. Reform Jews choose not to follow many of the ancient rules. Conservative Jews fall in between.

TEXTS LIST JEWISH BELIEFS

The laws and principles of Judaism are written down in sacred texts. The most important text is the **Torah**. The five books of the Torah record most of the laws and the history of Judaism until the death of Moses. Every **synagogue**, or place of Jewish worship, has at least one Torah.

> Circle the name of the most important sacred Jewish text.

The Torah is one of the three parts of the Hebrew Bible, or Tanakh (tah-NAKH). The second part contains messages from **prophets**, people who are said to receive messages directly from God. The third part is a collection of poems, songs, stories, lessons, and histories.

The **Talmud** is a collection of commentaries, folktales, and stories written by scholars. These are intended to help people understand and analyze the laws described in the Hebrew Bible.

> What is in the Talmud?
> _____
> _____
> _____
> _____

SCROLLS REVEAL PAST BELIEFS

Another set of ancient texts, the **Dead Sea Scrolls**, was discovered in 1947. These scrolls, written by Jewish scholars about 2,000 years ago, contain commentaries and stories, and offer more information about ancient Jewish life.

JUDAISM AND LATER CULTURES

Jewish ideas have helped shape two other major world religions, Christianity and Islam. The Ten Commandments are reflected in our laws and in modern society's rules of behavior.

CHALLENGE ACTIVITY

Critical Thinking: Drawing Inferences Pretend you are a writer contributing to a modern-day Talmud of American life. Write a short story illustrating how one of the Ten Commandments is still followed today.

Interactive Reader and Study Guide

The Hebrews and Judaism

MAIN IDEAS

1. Revolt, defeat, and migration led to great changes in Jewish culture.
2. Because Jews settled in different parts of the world, two different cultural traditions formed.
3. Jewish traditions and holy days celebrate their traditions and religion.

Key Terms and People

Zealots Jews who rebelled against their Roman rulers

rabbis teachers who guide Jews in their religious lives

Passover a time for Jews to remember the Exodus

High Holy Days the two most sacred Jewish holidays, Rosh Hashanah and Yom Kippur

Section Summary

REVOLT, DEFEAT, AND MIGRATION

The teachings of Judaism helped unite the ancient Jews. But many Jews were unhappy with the Roman rule of Jerusalem. Tensions increased. Some Jews refused to obey Roman officials. In AD 66, a group called the **Zealots** (ze-LUHTS) led a rebellion against Rome. After four years of fierce fighting, the rebellion failed. The Jews' main temple was destroyed in AD 70. The Romans put down another Jewish rebellion 60 years later. After this uprising, Jews were banned from living in Jerusalem. So they migrated to other parts of the world.

> Underline when the Zealots revolted against Roman rule. Why did they revolt?
>
> _____
>
> _____
>
> _____

TWO CULTURAL TRADITIONS

Because Jews could not worship at a central temple anymore, their traditions changed. Everywhere Jews went, they built local temples. They also appointed **rabbis**, religious leaders responsible for teaching Judaism. Even with a similar culture and

> Underline the definition of a rabbi in your summary.

background, Jewish traditions grew differently depending on where they moved. Two major Jewish cultures developed that still exist today.

The Ashkenazim (ahsh-kuh-NAH-zuhm) are descended from Jews who moved to France, Germany, and Eastern Europe. These Jews maintained separate customs from the region's residents. They even developed their own language, called Yiddish.

> **What was the main difference between the Ashkenazim and the Sephardim?**
> _____
> _____
> _____
> _____
> _____

The Sephardim (suh-FAHR-duhm) moved to Spain and Portugal. Unlike the Ashkenazim, these Jews mixed with their non-Jewish neighbors. This melding of language and culture produced a Jewish golden age in Spain and Portugal. Many Jews contributed to artistic achievement and scientific discovery.

TRADITIONS AND HOLY DAYS

No matter where Jews live, common traditions and holy days help them maintain and celebrate their long history. Many of these holidays honor the Jews' freedom. **Passover**, for example, celebrates the Jews' flight from slavery in Egypt during the Exodus. Hanukkah commemorates the successful rededication of the Temple of Jerusalem during the successful revolt against the Greeks in 160 BC.

The most important holidays are the **High Holy Days**. These holy days are Rosh Hashanah (rahsh-uh-SHAH-nuh), which celebrates the Jewish New Year, and Yom Kippur (yohm-ki-POOHR), when Jews ask God to forgive their sins.

> **What is the proper name for the Jewish New Year?**
> _____
> _____

CHALLENGE ACTIVITY

Critical Thinking: Drawing Inferences Pretend that you are a Jew being forced to leave Jerusalem during Roman rule. Where would you go—Spain or Portugal, or Eastern Europe? Write a letter to your relatives explaining why you chose a particular place. Be sure to refer to the differences between the Ashkenazim and Sephardim.

Ancient Greece

CHAPTER SUMMARY

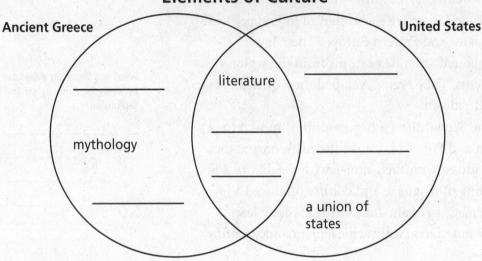

Comparing Important Elements of Culture

Ancient Greece   **United States**

literature

_____

_____

mythology   _____

_____

_____   a union of states

COMPREHENSION AND CRITICAL THINKING

Use the answers to the following questions to fill in the graphic organizer above.

1. Explain How is modern society similar to Ancient Greece? How is it different?

_____

_____

2. Identify Cause and Effect When and why did the Greeks form city-states?

_____

_____

3. Evaluate How did democracy first develop in Athens?

_____

4. Draw a Conclusion How did mythology influence the daily lives of Greeks?

_____

_____

Ancient Greece

> **MAIN IDEAS**
> 1. Geography helped shape early Greek civilizations.
> 2. Trading cultures developed in the Minoan and Mycenaean civilizations.
> 3. The Greeks created city-states for protection and security.

Key Terms and People

polis Greek word for city-state

classical filled with great achievements

acropolis a fortress atop a tall hill in the center of the city-states

Section Summary

GEOGRAPHY SHAPES GREEK CIVILIZATION

The Greeks lived on rocky, mountainous lands, located on a peninsula surrounded by the Mediterranean, Ionian, and Aegean Seas. The peninsula has an irregular shape. Many islands float off the mainland. This area was the home of one of the world's greatest civilizations.

> Underline the names of the three seas that ringed the Greek peninsula.

The few small valleys and plains of Greece provided farmland and that is where people settled. These communities were separated by steep mountains, so there was little contact between groups. The villages created separate governments.

> Why did separate governments develop in ancient Greece?
> _____
> _____
> _____

Because they were surrounded by water the Greeks became skilled shipbuilders and sailors. The Greeks were exposed to other cultures when they sailed to other lands.

TRADING CULTURES DEVELOP

Of the many cultures that settled and grew in early Greece, the earliest and most influential were the Minoans and the Mycenaens. By 2000 BC these two cultures had built advanced societies on the

Interactive Reader and Study Guide

island of Crete. The Minoans were known as the best shipbuilders of their time. They used ships mainly for trading purposes. A volcano that erupted in the 1600s BC may have led to the end of the Minoan civilization.

| While the Minoans built
_____,
the Mycenaeans built
_____. |

The Mycenaeans spoke the language that became Greek. While the Minoans were sailing, the Mycenaeans were building fortresses on the Greek mainland. The Mycenaeans eventually took over the trade routes once sailed by the Minoans. The Mycenaeans set up a powerful trading network on the Mediterranean and Black seas. But Mycenaean culture also fell prey to earthquakes and invaders. Greece entered a dark period.

GREEKS CREATE CITY-STATES

After 300 years of war and disorder communities began to band together for stability and protection. They created the **polis**, or city-state. This marked the beginning of the Greek **classical** age, a time filled with great achievements.

| What features of the polis made it a safe, protected place to live and conduct business?
_____
_____
_____ |

A city-state often was built around a fortress perched atop a high hill called an **acropolis**. Walls surrounded many of these cities. Much of daily life centered around the agora, or marketplace, where politics and shopping shared the stage. As stability returned some of the Greek city-states formed colonies in foreign lands. Early colonies included modern-day Istanbul in Turkey, Marseilles in France, and Naples in Italy. This created further independence for these city-states, and some city-states became great trading centers.

CHALLENGE ACTIVITY

Critical Thinking: Drawing Inferences You are a leader of an ancient Greek polis, or city-state, dealing with all the same problems and circumstances the real city-states of the time faced. Write your own set of laws that would improve both security and quality of life for the citizens who live there.

Ancient Greece

MAIN IDEAS

1. Aristocrats and tyrants ruled early Athens.
2. Athens created the world's first democracy.
3. Ancient democracy was different than modern democracy.

Key Terms and People

democracy type of government in which people rule themselves

oligarchy government in which only a few people have power

aristocrats rich landowners

citizens people with the right to participate in government

tyrant leader who rules by the use of force

Pericles Athenian leader who ruled at the height of Athenian democracy

Section Summary

ARISTOCRATS AND TYRANTS RULE

Democracy was born in Ancient Greece in the city of Athens. Democracy is a form of a government in which people rule themselves. However, Athens was ruled first by kings, and then by an **oligarchy** of **aristocrats**, or rich landowners.

In the 600s BC a group of rebels tried to overthrow the aristocrats. The rebellion failed and Draco gained power in Athens. Draco was a strict leader and was very unpopular. His successor, Solon, ruled that all free men were **citizens** who had a right to participate in government. But it was too late; people were tired of the aristocracy.

Peisistratus overthrew the oligarchy and became a leader of Athens by force. Peisistratus was the first **tyrant**. Though that word has a negative meaning today, some Greek tyrants were good leaders. Peisistratus led well and Athens flourished under his care. But after he died rebellious aristocrats regained control of Athens.

> Was democracy the only form of government in the ancient Greek city-states?
>
> _____
> _____

> Look up the word "draconian" in a dictionary. Write the definition here:
>
> _____
> _____
> _____
> _____

Interactive Reader and Study Guide

ATHENS CREATES DEMOCRACY

A leader named Cleisthenes introduced democracy to Athens in 500 BC. Though he was an aristocrat himself, he did not support the aristocracy. He overthrew the aristocratic leaders using popular support. Under his rule all citizens had the right to participate in the assembly that created laws. The assemblies were held outdoors and anyone could give a speech before votes were taken. This could be messy. Either too many people would come to an assembly or not enough. Eventually the Athenians began to select city officials to make decisions. Citizens were eventually allowed to decide court cases by serving on juries.

> **What do you think is the major disadvantage of allowing every citizen to participate in lawmaking?**
> _____
> _____
> _____
> _____

Citizens gradually gained more power. Athenian democracy reached its height with **Pericles**, who led the government from 460 to 429 BC. Still, democracy all but ended when Athens was conquered by Macedonia in the 330s BC. The Macedonian king did not like anyone other than himself making laws. Though the city council kept operating in a limited way, a new Greek king in 320 BC abolished even that right.

ANCIENT DEMOCRACY DIFFERS FROM MODERN DEMOCRACY

Although citizenship was very limited, Athens had a direct democracy, in which every citizen could participate and the majority ruled.

> **Name an example of direct democracy practiced in the United States today.**
> _____
> _____

The United States operates as a representative government, in which citizens elect people to represent them.

CHALLENGE ACTIVITY

Critical Thinking: Drawing Inferences Have students in the class discuss and vote on an issue—real or fictional—first as a direct democracy and then as a representative democracy. Have them discuss the merits of both democracies, or write a paper describing which system they prefer and why.

Ancient Greece

MAIN IDEAS

1. The Greeks created myths to explain the world.
2. Ancient Greek literature provides some of the world's greatest poems and stories.
3. Greek literature lives in and influences our world even today.

Key Terms and People

mythology body of stories about gods or heroes that tries to explain how the world works

Homer author of two great epic poems, the *Iliad* and the *Odyssey*

Sappho most famous lyrical poet of ancient Greece

Aesop author of the world's most famous set of fables

fables short stories that offer lessons on living

Section Summary

MYTHS EXPLAIN THE WORLD

Instead of science the ancient Greeks used **mythology**—stories about gods or heroes—to try to explain how the world works. The Greeks believed that the gods caused natural events, from the rising of the moon to thunderstorms. Everything was attributed to the gods, from disasters to daily events.

The Greeks believed that Demeter, the goddess of agriculture, caused the seasons. Hades, the god of the underworld, kidnapped Demeter's daughter. Demeter struck a bargain to get her daughter back for half of the year, during the spring and summer. In the winter, she missed her daughter, and because of her grief the plants did not grow.

Some myths told not of gods, but of heroes. Each city had its own hero, real or fictional, who would slay terrible monsters. The most famous Greek hero was Hercules. The Greeks loved to tell these stories.

> We often use the word "myth" as a synonym for "lie" or "untruth." Do you believe this is correct? Explain your answer.
>
> _____
> _____
> _____
> _____

> Is the story of Demeter worthless because it conflicts with the scientific explanation of seasonal change? Why or why not?
>
> _____
> _____
> _____

Section 3, *continued*

ANCIENT GREEK LITERATURE

Because of their love of stories, Greek writers produced great works of literature and some of the world's most famous stories. Among the earliest and most influential are the epic poems the *Iliad* and the *Odyssey*, by the poet **Homer**. It is thought that Homer lived some time during the 800s-700s BC. Scholars are not sure if Homer actually existed, but the poems were central to Greek lore and education. The *Iliad* told the story of the Myceaneans' war with the Trojans. The *Odyssey* told of the Greek hero Odysseus' long journey home after the war.

> If Homer did not exist, how do you think the *Iliad* and the *Odyssey* were composed?
>
> _____
> _____
> _____

Other forms of literature were also popular. Lyric poetry, recited by the poet while playing the lyre, was especially prized. The most famous lyric poet was a woman, **Sappho**. Fables, or short stories that offer the readers lessons on life, were also popular. The most famous fable writer was **Aesop**, who was said to live sometime before 400 BC. Aesop's fables are still commonly told today.

> Are there popular poets today who, like the ancient Greek lyric poets, perform their work while accompanying themselves with a stringed musical instrument? Can you name one?
>
> _____
> _____

GREEK LITERATURE LIVES

Greek literature, language, and art have had a great influence on modern culture. The English language is peppered with Greek expressions: a long journey, for example, is called an "odyssey" after Odysseus. Many places are named after Greek gods. Greek myths and stories have inspired painters, writers, and filmmakers for centuries.

> The Greek word for people is "demos." What political system is known in English by a word derived from "demos?"
>
> _____
> _____

CHALLENGE ACTIVITY

Critical Thinking: Drawing Inferences The later Greeks believed that their greatest literary works from earlier times were written by individual authors. Historical evidence suggests that these early works actually represented stories that evolved and changed with successive generations of poets. Write a paragraph describing why scholars might doubt the existence of writers like Homer and Aesop.

The Greek World

CHAPTER SUMMARY

Persia invades Greece

Athens-Sparta alliance victorious

Peloponnesian War between Athens and Sparta

Athenian culture flourishes

Alexander the Great captures Athens

Alexander's empire grows

Hellenistic culture flourishes

Rome engulfs Greece, Syria, and Egypt

COMPREHENSION AND CRITICAL THINKING

Use information from the graphic organizer to answer the following questions.

1. Recall Which ruler can be regarded as the founder of Hellenistic culture?

_____

2. Draw Inferences Why did the very different cultures of Athens and Sparta form an alliance?

_____

3. Evaluate Why do you think Athens surrendered so quickly to Alexander?

_____

4. Identify Which new major power put an end to Hellenistic culture?

_____

The Greek World

MAIN IDEAS
1. Persia became an empire under Cyrus the Great.
2. The Persian Empire grew stronger under Darius I.
3. The Persians fought Greece twice in the Persian Wars.

Key Terms and People

cavalry a unit of soldiers mounted on horses

Cyrus the Great founder of the Persian Empire

Darius I Persian emperor who organized and expanded the empire

Persian Wars a series of wars between Persia and Greece beginning in 490 BC

Xerxes I Persian emperor who led the second invasion of Greece in 480 BC

Section Summary

PERSIA BECOMES AN EMPIRE

Early in their history, the Persians often fought other peoples of Southwest Asia. In 550 BC the Persian king Cyrus II won independence from a group called the Medes. He went on to conquer almost all of Southwest Asia. His well-organized army included many war chariots and a powerful **cavalry**. Cyrus let the people he conquered keep their own customs. As a result, few people rebelled and the empire remained strong. By the time he died around 529 BC, Cyrus ruled the largest empire the world had ever seen. He became known in history as **Cyrus the Great**.

> What was the name of the people who lived in the region called Media?
> _____

THE PERSIAN EMPIRE GROWS STRONGER

Darius I seized power when the death of Cyrus's son left Persia without a clear leader. Darius organized the empire by dividing it into 20 provinces. Then he chose governors called satraps (SAY-traps) to rule the provinces for him.

> Why do you think king Cyrus became known as "the Great"?
> _____
> _____
> _____
> _____

Darius expanded the Persian Empire eastward to the Indus Valley and westward into Southeastern Europe. He called himself king of kings to remind other rulers of his power.

Darius's many improvements to Persian society included roads. Messengers used these roads to travel quickly throughout Persia. Darius also built a new capital called Persepolis.

During his reign a popular new religion called Zoroastrianism (zawr-uh-WAS-tree-uh-nih-zuhm) arose in Persia. This religion taught that the forces of good and evil were fighting for control of the universe.

> Do you think the Zoroastrian teaching is still relevant today? Why or why not?
> _____
> _____
> _____
> _____
> _____

THE PERSIANS FIGHT GREECE

In 499 BC several Greek cities in what is now Turkey rebelled against Persian rule. They were joined by a few city-states from mainland Greece. The Persians put down the revolt, but nine years later Darius invaded Greece and began the **Persian Wars**. The Greeks won the first battle, at Marathon, because they had better weapons and armor.

> Circle the sentence that explains why the Greeks defeated the Persians at the Battle of Marathon.

Ten years later, Persian Emperor **Xerxes I** (ZUHRK-seez) sent another army into Greece. The city-states of Athens and Sparta joined forces to defend Greece. Despite a brave stand by the Spartans at Thermopylae (thuhr-MAH-puh-lee), the Persians succeeded in attacking and burning Athens. However in the subsequent battles of Salamis (SAH-luh-muhs) and Plataea (pluh-TEE-uh), the Greeks prevailed and brought an end to the wars. They had defeated a powerful foe and defended their homeland.

> Who won the Persian Wars?

CHALLENGE ACTIVITY

Critical Thinking: Drawing Inferences Draw a simple map of a location where three armed soldiers could prevent an entire army of foot-soldiers from moving forward.

The Greek World

Section 2

MAIN IDEAS

1. The Spartans built a military society to provide security and protection.
2. The Athenians admired the mind and the arts in addition to physical abilities.
3. Sparta and Athens fought over who should have power and influence in Greece.

Key Terms and People

alliance an agreement to work together

Peloponnesian War a war between the two great Greek city-states of Athens and Sparta in the 400s BC

Section Summary

SPARTA BUILDS A MILITARY SOCIETY

Spartan life was dominated by the army. Courage and strength were the highest values. Unhealthy babies were taken outside the city and left to die. Boys who survived were trained from an early age to be soldiers. Boys ran, jumped, swam, and threw javelins to increase their strength. Men between the ages of 20 and 30 lived in army barracks and only occasionally visited their families. Spartan men stayed in the army until they turned 60.

Because Spartan men were often away at war, Spartan women had more rights than other Greek women. Women owned much of the land in Sparta and ran their households. Women also learned how to run, jump, wrestle, and throw javelins, and even competed with men in sporting events.

Slaves grew the city's crops and did many other jobs. Although slaves outnumbered Spartan citizens, fear of the army kept them from rebelling.

Sparta was officially ruled by two kings who jointly led the army. But elected officials ran

> Look up the word "Spartan" in a dictionary. Does it mean more than simply "having to do with Sparta?" Write that meaning here.
>
> _____
> _____
> _____
> _____
> _____

> If a baby could be taken by the government and left to die, what does this tell you about the real state of women's rights in Sparta?
>
> _____
> _____
> _____
> _____

Sparta's day-to-day activities and handled dealings between Sparta and other city-states.

ATHENIANS ADMIRE THE MIND

Sparta's main rival in Greece was Athens. Although Athens had a powerful military and valued physical training, the Athenians also prized education, clear thinking, and the arts. They believed that studying the arts made people better citizens.

> Underline the sentence that explains why the Athenians valued the arts.

In addition to physical training, many Athenian students learned to read, write, and count as well as sing and play musical instruments. Boys from rich families often had private tutors who taught them philosophy, geometry, astronomy, and other subjects, as well as public speaking. Boys from poor families, however, did not receive much education and girls got almost none. Despite Athens' reputation for freedom and democracy, Athenian women had almost no rights at all.

> Why do you think public speaking was considered an important part of the education of rich boys?
> _____
> _____
> _____

SPARTA AND ATHENS FIGHT

After the Persian Wars, many Greek city-states joined an **alliance** to help defend each other and protect trade. With its navy protecting the islands, Athens was the most powerful member of the league. Soon Athenians began to treat other city-states as their subjects. In 431 BC Sparta and other cities formed a league of their own and declared war on Athens. In the long **Peloponnesian War** that followed the Athenians won at first, but were forced to surrender in 404 BC. For about 30 years after this the Spartans controlled nearly all of Greece, but resentment from other city-states led to a long period of war that weakened all of Greece and left it open to attack from outside.

> Circle the noun that describes the popular feeling that undermined the power of Sparta.

CHALLENGE ACTIVITY

Critical Thinking: Drawing Inferences Write a poem or a song expressing how it feels when someone you love goes to fight in a war.

The Greek World

MAIN IDEAS

1. Macedonia conquered Greece in the 300s BC.
2. Alexander the Great built an empire that united much of Europe, Asia, and Egypt.
3. The Hellenistic kingdoms formed from Alexander's empire blended Greek and other cultures.

Key Terms and People

Philip II powerful king of Macedonia

phalanx a group of warriors who stood close together in a square

Alexander the Great king of Macedonia who built the largest empire the world had ever seen

Hellenistic name for the blended culture that developed in Alexander's empire

Section Summary

MACEDONIA CONQUERS GREECE

About 360 BC **Philip II** of Macedonia invaded Athens and won easily. The rest of Greece surrendered. Philip's victory resulted from his military strategy and weaponry. For instance, he extended the Greek idea of the **phalanx** by giving each soldier a spear 16 feet long. Philip planned to conquer Persia, but he was murdered in 336 BC and his throne passed to his 20-year-old son Alexander.

> Why do you think Philip's improvement on the phalanx gave his armies an advantage in battle?
>
> _____
> _____
> _____
> _____

ALEXANDER BUILDS AN EMPIRE

When Philip died, the people in the Greek city of Thebes rebelled. Alexander attacked Thebes and enslaved the Theban people. He used Thebes as an example of what would happen if any other Greek cities rebelled against him. Alexander went on to defeat the Persians time after time and to conquer Egypt. He became ruler of what had been the

> About what age was Alexander when his army attacked Thebes and enslaved the Thebans?

Interactive Reader and Study Guide

Section 3, *continued*

Persian empire. Before his death at 33 years of age, **Alexander the Great** (as he came to be called) had built an empire stretching from the Adriatic Sea west to India and to the Upper Nile in the south.

Alexander admired Greek culture and worked to spread Greek influence by founding cities in the lands he conquered. He encouraged Greek settlers to move to these new cities and as a result, Greek became a common language throughout Alexander's empire. Even as he supported the spread of Greek culture, however, Alexander encouraged common people to keep their own customs and traditions. The new, blended culture that developed is called **Hellenistic**. It was not purely Greek, but it was heavily influenced by Greek ideas.

> Underline the sentence that explains why Greek became a common language throughout Alexander's empire.

> Why is Hellenistic culture called a "blended" culture?
> _____
> _____
> _____
> _____

HELLENISTIC KINGDOMS

Alexander died unexpectedly without an obvious heir. With no clear direction, his generals fought for power. Eventually, three distinct Hellenistic kingdoms emerged: Macedonia (which included Greece), Syria, and Egypt. Although Hellenistic culture flourished in all three kingdoms—in particular, Alexandria in Egypt became a great center of culture and learning—all three kingdoms fell to the growing power of Rome between 60 and 30 BC.

> What new empire was growing in power during the 100s BC?
> _____
> _____

CHALLENGE ACTIVITY

Critical Thinking: Drawing Inferences Write a short essay that characterizes the United States as a blended culture.

Interactive Reader and Study Guide

The Greek World

MAIN IDEAS

1. The Greeks made great contributions to the arts.
2. The teachings of Socrates, Plato, and Aristotle are the basis of modern philosophy.
3. In science, the Greeks made key discoveries in math, medicine, and engineering.

Key Terms and People

Socrates the first of the great Greek thinkers and teachers

Plato teacher and thinker, student of Socrates, and founder of the Academy

Aristotle philosopher who taught that people should live lives of moderation based on reason

reason clear and ordered thinking

Euclid great and influential mathematician

Hippocrates great Greek doctor who taught how to treat disease by understanding what caused illness

Section Summary

THE ARTS

The ancient Greeks were master artists. Their paintings and statues have been admired for hundreds of years. Greek sculptors studied the human body, especially how it looks when it is moving. They used what they learned when they made their statues. Greek artists painted detailed scenes on vases, pots, and other vessels. The remains of Greek architecture show how much care the Greeks took in designing their buildings so they would reflect the beauty of their cities.

> **Which three art forms are mentioned in this paragraph?**
>
> _____
> _____
> _____
> _____

Greek writers created new literary forms, including drama and history. Dramatists wrote tragedies, which described hardships faced by Greek heroes, and comedies, which made fun of people and ideas.

Section 4, *continued*

Historians were interested in the lessons that history could teach. They tried to figure out what caused wars so the Greeks could learn from their mistakes and avoid similar wars in the future.

PHILOSOPHY

The ancient Greeks worshipped gods and goddesses whose actions explained many of the mysteries of the world. But around 500 BC a few people began to think about other explanations. We call these people philosophers. Philosophers believe in the power of the human mind to think, explain, and understand life.

> Look in a dictionary for the etymology (word origin) of the word "philosophy."

Socrates (SAHK-ruh-teez) believed that people must never stop looking for knowledge. He taught by asking questions. When people answered, he challenged their answers with more questions. His student **Plato** (PLAYT-oh) created a school called the Academy to which students, philosophers, and scientists could come to discuss ideas. Plato's student **Aristotle** (ar-uh-STAH-tuhl) taught that people should live lives of moderation, or balance. He believed that moderation was based on **reason**. Aristotle also made great advances in the field of logic, the process of making inferences.

> Would Socrates say that we stop learning when we leave school? What would he say?
>
> _____
> _____
> _____
> _____
> _____

SCIENCE

Many of the rules we still use today to measure and calculate were first developed by Greek mathematicians like **Euclid** (YOO-kluhd). Greek doctors like **Hippocrates** (hip-AHK-ruh-teez) wanted to cure diseases and keep people healthy. Greek inventors also made many discoveries that are still in use, from practical devices like water screws (which bring water up from a lower level to a higher one) to playful mechanical toys.

> Do you think doctors today have the same fundamental beliefs about medicine as Hippocrates did? Why or why not?
>
> _____
> _____
> _____
> _____

CHALLENGE ACTIVITY

Critical Thinking: Drawing Inferences Write a story, poem, or play that makes fun of some political figure.

Interactive Reader and Study Guide

The Roman Republic

CHAPTER SUMMARY

Patrician	Plebeian	The poor	Slave
wealthy	gained some political power	could not join the army	had no legal rights
original Roman Senate member	could eventually serve in a political position	could not vote	considered property of the wealthy
had most of the political power	could serve in the army	had very few rights	
could serve in any political position	could not marry a patrician		
could vote	later got the vote		

COMPREHENSION AND CRITICAL THINKING

Use information from the graphic organizer to answer the following questions.

1. **Explain** What class of people originally held all of the political power in Rome?

_____

2. **Identify Cause and Effect** Why did the patricians change the government and allow plebeians to run for political office?

_____

_____

3. **Evaluate** Who did not have the right to vote or participate in politics? Why?

_____

4. **Draw a Conclusion** Was Rome a fair place for most people who lived there, or were other ancient civilizations better? Why or why not?

_____

_____

The Roman Republic

MAIN IDEAS

1. The geography of Italy made land travel difficult but helped the Romans prosper.
2. Ancient historians were very interested in Rome's legendary history.
3. Once a monarchy, the Romans created a republic.

Key Terms and People

Aeneas mythical hero who fled the fallen city of Troy for Italy in a journey chronicled in Virgil's *Aeneid*

Romulus and Remus mythical twin brothers who are said to have founded Rome

republic government led by rulers elected by the citizens

dictator ruler with almost absolute power, elected during time of war

Cincinnatus famous dictator who chose not to retain his power

plebeians Rome's common people, including artisans, craftsmen, and traders

patricians wealthy, noble people of Rome

Section Summary

THE GEOGRAPHY OF ITALY

Rome grew from a small town on the Tiber River to become a great power. Rome conquered Greece, Mesopotamia, Egypt, and Persia. Rome's central location and good climate were factors in its success. Because most of Italy is surrounded by water, Romans could easily travel by sea. The mountains in the north made it difficult to travel over land. The warm dry weather resulted in high crop yields, so the Romans had plenty of food.

> Why do you think Italy's geography helped the rise of Rome?
>
> _____
>
> _____
>
> _____

ROME'S LEGENDARY ORIGINS

Rome's beginnings are a mystery. A few ancient ruins show that people lived there as early as 800 BC. Later, the Romans wanted a glorious past, so they created stories or legends about their history.

> Why did the Romans make up stories and legends about their history?
>
> _____
>
> _____
>
> _____

The early Romans believed their history began with the mythical hero **Aeneas** (i-NEE-uhs). Aeneas fled Troy when the Greeks destroyed the city during the Trojan War. He formed an alliance with a group called the Latins and traveled to Italy. This story is told in the *Aeneid* (i-NEE-id), an epic poem written by a poet named Virgil (VUHR-juhl) around 20 BC.

> **Why is Aeneas sometimes referred to as "the Father of Rome?"**
>
> _____
>
> _____
>
> _____

According to legend, Rome was built by twin brothers **Romulus** (RAHM-yuh-luhs) and **Remus** (REE-muhs). Romulus killed Remus and became the first king of Rome. Scholars believe Rome started sometime between 800 and 700 BC. Early Rome was ruled by kings until the Romans created a **republic** in 509 BC.

> **Which of the two brothers named the city of Rome after himself?**
>
> _____
>
> _____

THE EARLY REPUBLIC

In the republic the Romans created, citizens elected leaders to govern them. They voted once a year to prevent any one person from gaining too much power. But early Rome had its troubles. For one thing, Rome was usually at war with nearby countries.

To lead the country during war, the Romans elected **dictators**, rulers with almost absolute power. A dictator's power could not last more than six months. The most famous dictator was **Cincinnatus** (sin-suh-NAT-uhs), a farmer elected to defeat a major enemy. He resigned as dictator right after the war and went back to his farm.

Within Rome the **plebeians**, or common people, worked for change. Only the city's **patricians**, the wealthy citizens, could be elected to rule Rome. When the plebeians elected a council, the patricians changed the government.

> **Why do you think Rome's patricians were so concerned when the plebeians elected their own council?**
>
> _____
>
> _____
>
> _____
>
> _____

CHALLENGE ACTIVITY

Critical Thinking: Drawing Inferences You are a Roman plebeian. Write a campaign speech saying why people should elect you to office—even though your position has no official power. Create a historically accurate persona.

The Roman Republic

MAIN IDEAS

1. Roman government was made up of three parts that worked together to run the city.
2. Written laws helped keep order in Rome.
3. The Roman Forum was the heart of Roman society.

Key Terms and People

magistrates officials elected to fulfill specific duties for the city

consuls most powerful elected officials in the Roman Republic

Roman Senate a powerful group of wealthy citizens who advised elected officials

veto to prohibit an official action

Latin language spoken by the ancient Romans

checks and balances methods of balancing power

forum Rome's public meeting place

Section Summary

ROMAN GOVERNMENT

During the 400s BC, the plebeians were unhappy that they did not have any say with the government. The city's leaders knew that they had to compromise or the plebeians might rise up and overthrow the government. So the patricians created positions in the government for the plebeians. A tripartite (try-PAHR-tyt) government, a government with three parts, was established to keep any one group from getting too much power.

The first part of the government was made up elected officials called **magistrates** (MA-juh-strayts). The most powerful magistrates were called **consuls** (KAHN-suhlz). Two consuls were elected each year to run the city and lead the army. The consuls got advice from the **Roman Senate**. The Senate was a council of wealthy, powerful citizens who held seats for life. Magistrates who finished their one-year terms

Why do you think it is important to keep too much power from concentrating among one group of people?

_____

_____

_____

What is the difference between a consul and a magistrate?

_____

_____

_____

earned a seat on the Senate, so the Senate gained more power as time passed.

The third branch of government had two parts. The first branch was made up of assemblies. The assemblies elected the magistrates who ran the city of Rome. The second branch was a group of officials called tribunes. The tribunes had the power to **veto** (VEE-toh), or prohibit, actions by the government. Veto means "to forbid" in **Latin**, the ancient Roman language.

Checks and balances existed to even out power. Some officials had the power to block actions by other officials. Action could be stalled if people could not work together. But when an agreement was reached, Rome worked strongly and efficiently.

> Underline the definition of the Latin word "veto."

WRITTEN LAWS KEEP ORDER

At first Rome's laws were not written down. People thought that it was not fair to be charged by laws they did not know existed. In 450 BC Rome's first legal code was written on twelve bronze tablets and displayed in the **forum**, Rome's public meeting place. Although the Romans continued to make laws, the Law of the Twelve Tables remained as the basis of Roman law.

> What was the official name of Rome's first set of written laws?
>
> _____
> _____
> _____

THE ROMAN FORUM

The forum was the heart of Rome. All the important government buildings and religious temples were there. It was also the main meeting place for Roman citizens. It was used for public speeches, and for shopping and entertainment.

> Do you think our modern idea of "downtown" is related to the idea of the Roman Forum? Why or why not?
>
> _____
> _____
> _____
> _____

CHALLENGE ACTIVITY

Critical Thinking: Drawing Inferences Do some research and locate the text of the Roman law code of 450 BC. Which laws do you think were fair and which laws do you think were unfair? Remove and change any unfair laws, explaining how and why you made the changes. Discuss whether those laws, including the amended ones, should or should not apply to the modern world.

The Roman Republic

MAIN IDEAS
1. The late republic period saw the growth of territory and trade.
2. Through wars, Rome grew beyond Italy.
3. Several crises struck the republic in its later years.

Key Terms and People

legions groups of up to 6,000 soldiers

Punic Wars a series of wars between Rome and Carthage

Hannibal brilliant Carthaginian general who attacked the city of Rome

Gaius Marius general who tried to solve unemployment by inviting poor people to join the army, creating a force more loyal to him than to Rome

Lucius Cornelius Sulla rival of Marius who raised his own army to defeat Marius and take control of Rome

Spartacus slave and former gladiator who led an uprising of slaves

Section Summary

GROWTH OF TERRITORY AND TRADE

Rome expanded due to threats from other cities. When the Gauls took over Rome in 410 BC, Roman officials paid them to leave. Because of this Rome was constantly fighting off invaders. Rome's army was very organized, so defense of the city was usually successful. Soldiers were divided into **legions**, or groups of up to 6,000 men. Each legion was divided into centuries, or groups of 100 soldiers. The army had the flexibility to fight together, or break up into smaller groups.

Most Romans were originally farmers. Many of them moved to the city and ran their farms from afar with help from slaves. As the population of the city grew, so did the need for more food. An extensive trading network was established. Rome coined copper and silver money, which was used widely in the region.

> What is the military advantage of an army with both small units and large units?
>
> _____
> _____
> _____
> _____

> What necessity led to the expansion of trade in ancient Rome?
>
> _____
> _____

Interactive Reader and Study Guide

ROME GROWS BEYOND ITALY

Rome's growth made both allies and enemies in the Mediterranean. The Roman army fought many wars, including the **Punic** (PYOO-nik) **Wars** with Carthage. Carthage was the capital of a Phoenician civilization that flourished in North Africa between 264 and 156 BC. Although an attack on Rome led by the brilliant general **Hannibal** nearly succeeded, Rome eventually conquered Carthage. The Romans then took over Gaul, Greece, and parts of Asia. The Romans were deeply influenced by the Greeks and adopted much of the Greek culture.

> **What body of water lay between Rome and Carthage?**
> _____
> _____

CRISES STRIKE THE REPUBLIC

As Rome's territory grew, so did its problems. Tensions between the rich and poor grew. Some leaders tried to keep the poor citizens happy, but their plans were not popular with the wealthy. Politicians who tried to make a change and went against Rome's powerful leaders were killed.

Army general **Gaius Marius** (GY-uhs MER-ee-uhs) encouraged the poor and the unemployed to join the army. Before, only people who owned property had been allowed in the army. As a result, the army became more loyal to Marius than to the Roman government.

> **Why do you think the poor and unemployed respected Gaius Marius?**
> _____
> _____
> _____

Another man, **Lucius Cornelius Sulla** (LOO-shuhs kawr-NEEL-yuhs SUHL-uh), raised his own army. He fought and killed Marius and became dictator. Soon afterward, **Spartacus** (SPAHR-tuh-kuhs), a slave and former gladiator, led an uprising of thousands of slaves against the republic. Spartacus was eventually defeated and killed, but these conflicts had weakened Rome.

> **Why do you think Spartacus attracted such a large following?**
> _____
> _____
> _____

CHALLENGE ACTIVITY

Critical Thinking: Drawing Inferences Spartacus was eventually caught and killed, yet his rebellion had an impact on Roman history. Write an essay evaluating how one person can affect the course of history, using Spartacus as an example.

Rome and Christianity

CHAPTER SUMMARY

History of the Roman Empire

	Western Empire	Eastern Empire
Capital		Constantinople
Description of Religion		Eastern Orthodox Church
Date of fall	476	
Conquered by	Goths and other barbarians	

COMPREHENSION AND CRITICAL THINKING

Use the answers to the following questions to fill in the graphic organizer above.

1. Describe Give one example of Roman architecture, one example of Roman art, and one example of Roman literature.

_____

2. Explain Who was the Messiah? Why did Jews think he was important?

_____

3. Evaluate Why do you think some Roman emperors persecuted Christians?

_____

_____

4. Draw a Conclusion Why do you think Rome eventually adopted Christianity, which was once illegal in the Roman Empire, as Rome's official religion?

_____

_____

5. Identify Cause and Effect When did the eastern empire fall? Why did the eastern empire last longer than the western empire?

_____

_____

The Roman Empire and Christianity

Section 1

> **MAIN IDEAS**
> 1. Disorder in the Roman Republic created an opportunity for Julius Caesar to gain power.
> 2. The Republic ended when Augustus became Rome's first empire.
> 3. The Roman Empire grew to control the entire Mediterranean world.
> 4. The Romans accomplished great things in science, engineering, architecture, art, literature, and law.

Key Terms and People

Cicero orator who said Romans should give control of government back to the Senate

orator a public speaker

Julius Caesar the greatest general in Roman history

Augustus Caesar's adopted son, defeated Antony and Cleopatra

provinces the areas outside of Italy that the Romans controlled

currency money

Pax Romana the Roman Peace, a peaceful period in Rome's history

aqueduct a raised channel used to carry water from mountains into cities

Ovid a poet who wrote about Roman mythology

Romance languages the languages that developed from Latin

civil law a legal system based on a written code of laws

Academic Vocabulary

agreement a decision reached by two or more people or groups

Section Summary

DISORDER AND THE END OF THE REPUBLIC

Cicero, a famous **orator**, asked Romans to return power to the Senate and bring order back to Rome. But Rome's government stayed the same.

After conquering Gaul and defeating Pompey, **Julius Caesar** named himself Roman dictator. But on March 15 in 44 BC, a group of Senators stabbed him to death. **Marc Antony** and Octavian, later renamed **Augustus**, took charge of Roman politics. They defeated Caesar's killers, who then killed

> **What actions did Cicero ask Romans to take?**
> _____
> _____

Interactive Reader and Study Guide

themselves. Octavian returned to Italy while Antony headed east to fight Rome's enemies.

In Egypt Antony fell in love with Cleopatra and was named king of Egypt. Antony divorced Octavian's sister. In 31 BC Octavian defeated Antony's fleet. Antony escaped and returned to Cleopatra. They killed themselves to avoid capture.

> Circle the two sentences that best explains why Octavian sent a fleet to attack Antony.

Octavian ruled Rome. He claimed that he was giving his power to the Senate. But he took the name Augustus and became the Roman emperor.

ROME'S GROWING EMPIRE

By the 100s, the Romans ruled Gaul and much of central Europe. Their empire stretched from Asia Minor to Britain. Traders traveled the **provinces** to trade artisans' goods for metals, cloth, and food. Roman coins were used all over as **currency**. The **Pax Romana** was a time of peace and prosperity.

ROME'S ACCOMPLISHMENTS

Romans took a practical approach to engineering and science. They improved on Greek medicine. They made lasting structures with cement and arches. Roman **aqueducts** still stand today. Romans used vaults to create open spaces in buildings.

> Why do you think some Roman structures still stand?
> _____
> _____
> _____

The Romans prized beauty. Greek designs influenced their art and architecture. Romans decorated walls with frescoes and floors with mosaics. Many sculptors copied Greek sculptures.

> How were the Romans influenced by the Greeks?
> _____
> _____
> _____

Ovid wrote lovely poems, and Virgil wrote a great epic, the *Aeneid,* about the founding of Rome. Roman poets wrote in Latin. Latin later led to the development of the **Romance languages**.

Civil law was inspired by Roman law, which was enforced throughout the Roman Empire. Most European nations today are ruled by civil law.

CHALLENGE ACTIVITY

Critical Thinking: Summarizing Summarize the events leading from Caesar's conquest of Gaul to Octavian's becoming Roman emperor.

Rome and Christianity

Section 2

> **MAIN IDEAS**
> 1. Romans generally practiced religious tolerance, but they came into conflict with the Jews.
> 2. A new religion, Christianity, grew out of Judaism.
> 3. Jesus of Nazareth, who preached about salvation, love for God, and kindness was seen as the Messiah by many.
> 4. Christianity grew in popularity and eventually became the sole religion allowed in the Roman Empire.

Key Terms and People

Christianity religion based on the teachings of Jesus of Nazareth

Jesus of Nazareth founder of Christianity

Messiah leader Jews believed would return and restore the greatness of Israel

Bible the holy book of Christianity

crucifixion a type of execution that involved being nailed to a cross

Resurrection Christian belief that Jesus rose from the dead three days after his death

disciples followers

Apostles the 12 disciples whom Jesus chose to receive special teaching

Paul of Tarsus disciple whose letters defined Christianity as separate from Judaism

martyrs people who die for their religious beliefs

persecution punishing people for their beliefs

Constantine Roman emperor who became a Christian

Section Summary

RELIGIOUS TOLERANCE AND CONFLICT

Rome conquered Judea, the homeland of most Jews, in 63 BC. Roman leaders banned a religion only if there were political problems. Some Romans felt the Jewish belief in one god insulted their gods. But Judaism was not banned at first. The Jews wanted to be free, so they rebelled. In the end, Rome sacked the capital Jerusalem and forced the Jews to scatter.

> Why do you think the Romans usually chose to tolerate the religions of conquered peoples?
>
> _____
> _____
> _____
> _____

A NEW RELIGION

At the start of the first century AD, a new religion appeared. **Christianity** had roots in Judaism, but it was based on the teachings of **Jesus of Nazareth**.

At this time there were several Jewish groups. The largest group followed Moses's laws very strictly to ensure that a savior would appear. This savior was called the **Messiah** (muh-SY-uh), which means "God's chosen one." When Judea had fallen, many Jews felt the Messiah would come soon.

Jesus of Nazareth was born at the end of the first century BC. Much of what we know about Jesus is from the **Bible**, the holy book of Christianity. Jesus was born in Bethlehem (BETH-li-hem) to a woman named Mary. Christians believe that God was Jesus's father. When Jesus was about 30, he began to travel and teach. Roman leaders thought his teachings challenged their authority. Jesus was arrested and executed by **crucifixion**. Christians believe Jesus rose from the dead. This is called the **Resurrection**. Many of Jesus's **disciples** claimed to see him again.

Jesus taught that people should love God and each other. Jesus also taught about salvation. Jesus chose 12 of his disciples, the **Apostles**, to spread his teachings. However another man, **Paul of Tarses**, was most important in spreading Christianity. Paul traveled and wrote letters explaining Christianity. He helped Christianity break away from Judaism.

THE GROWTH OF CHRISTIANITY

As Christianity became more popular, Roman leaders began to worry. Christians began preaching to Jews and non-Jews. Some local leaders arrested and killed Christians. These **martyrs** died for their religious beliefs. Some Roman emperors outlawed Christianity and **persecuted** Christians.

In the early 300s, emperor **Constantine** became a Christian and removed the bans on Christians. Later Christianity became the official religion of Rome.

CHALLENGE ACTIVITY

Critical Thinking: Drawing Inferences How did Emperor Hadrian deal with religious rebels? Would you do the same? Explain why or why not.

> Why do you think the Messiah was so important for the Jews who were living in Judea under Roman rule?
>
> _____
> _____
> _____
> _____

> Do you think modern leaders who say they are Christians act with Jesus's teachings in mind? Why or why not? Provide examples to support your opinion.
>
> _____
> _____
> _____
> _____

> Why do you think the early Christians were slow to offer their message to non-Jews?
>
> _____
> _____
> _____
> _____

Rome and Christianity

MAIN IDEAS

1. Many problems threatened the Roman Empire, leading one emperor to divide it in half.

2. Rome declined because of barbarian invasion and political and economic problems.

3. In the eastern empire, people created a new society and religious traditions that were very different from those in the west.

Key Terms and People

Diocletian emperor who divided the Roman Empire into two parts

Attila fearsome Hun leader who attacked Rome's eastern empire

corruption decay in people's values

Justinian last ruler of the Roman Empire

Theodora Justinian's wife, a wise woman who advised her husband during his reign

Byzantine Empire civilization that developed in the eastern Roman Empire

Academic Vocabulary

efficient productive and not wasteful

Section Summary

PROBLEMS IN THE EMPIRE

At its height the Roman Empire ruled all of the land around the Mediterranean Sea. But by the late 100s, emperors had to give up some land.

Rome had to defend itself constantly from attacks from the north and the east. Problems came from within the empire, too. Disease killed many people. Taxes were high. Food was scarce because many farmers went to war. To increase food production, Germanic farmers were invited to work on Roman lands, but they were not loyal to Rome.

The emperor **Diocletian** took power in the late 200s. He ruled the east himself and chose a co-emperor to rule the west. The emperor Constantine reunited the empire for a short time. He moved the capital from Rome to Constantinople in the east.

> Name three problems facing the Roman Empire around 200.
> _____
> _____
> _____

> Do you think Diocletian's decision to divide the Roman Empire made sense? Why or why not?
> _____
> _____
> _____
> _____

THE DECLINE OF ROME

Once the capital moved to the east, barbarians attacked Roman territory in the north. During the late 300s, an Asian group called the Huns began attacking the Goths. The Goths were forced into Roman territory. In the end, the Goths broke through into Italy and destroyed Rome.

The Vandals, Angles, Saxons, Jutes, and Franks all invaded Roman territory in the west. The Huns under **Attila** raided in the east. In 476 a barbarian leader overthrew the Roman emperor and became king. This ended the western empire.

The vast size of the Roman empire also contributed to its fall. The government was not **efficient**, and it suffered from **corruption**. Rome was no longer the great center it had once been.

> A famous phrase says "power corrupts and absolute power corrupts absolutely." Do you think this is true? Why or why not?
> _____
> _____
> _____
> _____

A NEW EASTERN EMPIRE

As Rome fell, the eastern empire prospered. **Justinian** ruled the east in the 500s. He wanted to reunite the Roman Empire. His armies recaptured Italy. He was respected for making laws more fair. But he made enemies who tried to overthrow him. Justinian got advice from his wife **Theodora** and was able to keep his throne. Despite Justinian's success, the empire declined for 700 years. In 1453 Constantinople was defeated by the Ottoman Turks.

> Who was Justinian's most trusted advisor?
> _____
> _____

People in the eastern empire began to follow non-Roman influences. The **Byzantine Empire** developed in the east. This empire practiced Christianity differently than Romans. In the 1000s, the church split in two. In the east the Eastern Orthodox Church formed. Thus religion further divided eastern and western Europe.

> Some historians believe that the well-known historical division between the "eastern" and "western" worlds begins in Byzantine culture. Do you think this so? Why or why not?
> _____
> _____
> _____
> _____
> _____

CHALLENGE ACTIVITY

Critical Thinking: Drawing Inferences Was there anything the rulers could have done to stop the disintegration of the Roman empire, or was it inevitable? Write a one-page essay explaining your answer.

Interactive Reader and Study Guide

The Islamic World

CHAPTER SUMMARY

Examples of Islamic Impact

	Western Empire
Arabia	First caliph unified Arabia for first time
Social Change	
Role of Women	
Byzantine Empire	Overcame by Ottoman Turks
Science, Medicine, and Mathematics	
Arts and Architecture	*The Thousand and One Nights*, Taj Mahal

COMPREHENSION AND CRITICAL THINKING

Use the answers to the following questions to fill in the graphic organizer above.

1. Explain Who was the first caliph? What did he accomplish?

_____

_____

2. Identify Cause and Effect How did the teachings of Muhammad affect early Arabian society?

_____

_____

3. Evaluate Name three great achievements of Islamic empires.

_____

_____

4. Draw a Conclusion Were the Islamic empires a good place to live if you were a woman or a non-Muslim? Explain.

_____

_____

The Islamic World

MAIN IDEAS

1. Arabia is a mostly a desert land where two ways of life, nomadic and sedentary, developed

2. A new religion called Islam, founded by the prophet Muhammad, spread throughout Arabia in the 600s.

Key Terms and People

oasis a wet, fertile area in the desert

caravan a group of traders that travels together

Muhammad an Arabian prophet whose teachings became the basis for a new religion

Islam religion based on messages Muhammad received from God

Muslim a person who follows Islam

Qur'an the holy book of Islam

pilgrimage journey to a sacred place

mosque a building for Muslim prayer

Academic Vocabulary

influence change, or have an effect on

Section Summary

LIFE IN A DESERT LAND

Arabia, in the southwest corner of Asia, is the crossroads for Africa, Europe, and Asia. Arabia is a mostly hot and dry desert of scorching temperatures and little water. Water is scarce and exists mainly in oases. An **oasis** is a wet, fertile area in the desert. Oases are key stops along Arabia's trade routes.

People developed two ways to live in the desert. Nomads moved from place to place. Nomads lived in tents and raised goats, sheep, and camels. They traveled with their herds to find food and water for their animals. They traveled in tribes, or groups of people. Tribe membership provided protection from danger and reduced competition for grazing lands.

> Arabia was the trading crossroads for what three continents?
> _____
> _____
> _____
> _____

> Why would a nomad prefer to travel in a tribe?
> _____
> _____
> _____
> _____

Others led a settled life. Towns sprang up in oases along the trade routes. Merchants and craftspeople traded with groups of traders who traveled together in **caravans**. Most towns had a market or bazaar. Both nomads and caravans used these centers of trade.

A NEW RELIGION

A man named **Muhammad** brought a new religion to Arabia. Much of what we know about him comes from religious writings. Muhammad was born in the city of Mecca around 570. As a child, he traveled with his uncle's caravans. As an adult, Muhammad managed a caravan business.

> Circle the name of Islam's prophet and founder.

Muhammad was upset that rich people did not help the poor. He often went to a cave to meditate on this problem. According to Islamic belief, when Muhammad was 40, an angel spoke to him. These messages form the basis of a religion called **Islam**. They were written in the **Qur´an** (kuh-RAN), the holy book of Islam. A follower of Islam is called a **Muslim**.

> Where did Muhammad first hear from an angel of God?
> _____
> _____

Muhammad taught that there was only one God, Allah. The belief in one god was a new idea for many Arabs. Before this time, Arabs prayed to many gods at shrines. The most important shrine was in Mecca. Many people traveled to Mecca every year on a **pilgrimage**. Muhammad also taught that the rich should give money to the poor. But rich merchants in Mecca rejected this idea.

> Why do you think the rich merchants disliked being told they should give money to the poor?
> _____
> _____
> _____
> _____

Slowly, Muhammad's message began to **influence** people. The rulers in Mecca felt threatened by him. Muhammed left and went to Medina. His house there became the first **mosque**, or building for Muslim prayer. After years of conflict, the people of Mecca finally gave in and accepted Islam.

CHALLENGE ACTIVITY

Critical Thinking: Drawing Inferences If you lived in Arabia, would you choose a nomadic or sedentary life? Write a one-page description of what your life would be like.

The Islamic World

> **MAIN IDEAS**
> 1. The Qur'an guides Muslims' lives.
> 2. The Sunnah tells Muslims of important duties expected of them.
> 3. Islamic law is based on the Qur'an and the Sunnah.

Key Terms and People

jihad literally means "to make an effort" or "to struggle"
Sunnah a collection of actions or sayings by Muhammad
Five Pillars of Islam the five acts of worship required of all Muslims

Section Summary

THE QUR'AN

After Muhammad died, his followers wrote down all of the messages he received from Allah. This collection of teachings became known as the Qur'an. Muslims believe that the Qur'an is the exact word of God as it was told to Muhammad. Like the Jewish and Christian bibles, the Qur'an says there is one God (Allah). Islam teaches that there is a definite beginning and end to the world. On that final day, Muslims believe, God will judge all people. Those who have obeyed God's orders will be granted life in paradise. Those who have not obeyed God will be punished.

> Circle the name of Islam's most important holy book.

Muslims believe that God wishes them to follow many rules in order to be judged a good person. These rules affect the everyday life of Muslims. In the early days of Islam, these rules led to great changes in Arabian society. For example, owning slaves was forbidden.

Jihad (ji-HAHD) is an important Islamic concept. Literally, jihad means "to make an effort" or "to struggle." It refers to the internal struggle of a Muslim trying to follow Islamic beliefs. It can also mean the struggle to defend the Muslim community

> How do you think "jihad" came to mean "holy war?"
> _____
> _____
> _____
> _____

or convert people to Islam. The word has also been translated as "holy war."

THE SUNNAH

Another important holy book in Islam is the **Sunnah** (SOOH-nuh), a collection of Muhammad's words and actions. The Sunnah spells out the main duties for Muslims. These are known as the **Five Pillars of Islam**. The first pillar is a statement of faith. The second pillar says a Muslim must pray five times daily. The third pillar is a yearly donation to charity. The fourth pillar is fasting during the holy month of Ramadan (RAH-muh-dahn). The fifth pillar is the hajj (HAJ), a pilgrimage to Mecca. The hajj must be made at least once in a lifetime.

The Sunnah also preaches moral duties that must be met in daily life, in business, and in government. For example, it is considered immoral to owe someone money or to disobey a leader.

> **Do Muslims believe that the Sunnah is the direct word of God?**
> _____
> _____

> **What is the third pillar of Islam?**
> _____
> _____
> _____
> _____

ISLAMIC LAW

The Qur'an and the Sunnah form the basis of Islamic law, or Shariah (shuh-REE-uh). Shariah lists rewards or punishments for obeying or disobeying laws. Shariah punishments can be severe. Shariah makes no distinction between religious and secular life. Most Islamic countries today blend Islamic law with a legal system much like that in the United States.

> **Is Shariah the only law used in Islamic countries?**
> _____
> _____
> _____
> _____

CHALLENGE ACTIVITY

Critical Thinking: Drawing Inferences Write a brief essay evaluating the differences and similarities between the two earlier religions of Judaism and Christianity with Islam. Focus not only on beliefs but also on practices and what social conditions might have influenced these practices in all the religions.

The Islamic World

MAIN IDEAS

1. Muslim armies conquered many lands into which Islam slowly spread.
2. Trade helped Islam spread into new areas.
3. Three Muslim empires controlled much of Europe, Asia, and Africa from the 1400s to the 1800s.

Key Terms and People

Abu Bakr one of Islam's first converts, appointed caliph after Muhammad's death

caliph title of the highest Islamic leader

tolerance acceptance

Janissaries slave boys converted to Islam and trained as soldiers

Mehmed II Ottoman ruler who defeated the Byzantine Empire

Suleyman I Ottoman ruler who led the empire to its heights

Shia Muslims who believed only members of Muhammad's family should be caliphs

Sunni Muslims who believed caliphs did not have to be related to Muhammad

Academic Vocabulary

development the process of growing or improving

Section Summary

MUSLIMS ARMIES CONQUER MANY LANDS

After Muhammad's death **Abu Bakr** (uh-boo bak-uhr) was the leader of Islam. He was the first **caliph** (kay-luhf). This title was used for the highest Islamic leader. Abu Bakr unified Arabia. The Arab army conquered the Persian and Byzantine empires.

Later caliphs conquered lands in Central Asia, northern India, and North Africa. They controlled eastern Mediterranean trade routes. After many years of fighting, the Berbers of North Africa converted to Islam. A combined Arab and Berber army conquered Spain and ruled for 700 years.

> What present-day countries mark the eastern and western boundaries of the Islamic empire?
>
> _____
> _____
> _____

> Why do think trade flourishes in coastal cities?
>
> _____
> _____
> _____

TRADE HELPS ISLAM SPREAD

Arab merchants took Islamic beliefs and practices with them to new lands. Coastal trading cities

Interactive Reader and Study Guide

developed into large Muslim communities.

Muslims generally practiced **tolerance**, or acceptance. They did not ban all other religions in their lands. More people began speaking Arabic and practicing Islam. The Arabs also took on non-Muslim customs. Cultural blending changed Islam into a religion of many cultures. The **development** of Muslim cities like Baghdad and Córdoba reflected this blending of cultures.

THREE MUSLIM EMPIRES

In the 1200s, Muslim Turks known as Ottomans attacked the Byzantine Empire. They trained **Janissaries**, boys from conquered towns who were enslaved and converted to Islam. The Janissaries fought fiercely. In 1453 the Ottomans led by **Mehmed II** took Constantinople. This ended the Byzantine Empire. The Ottoman Empire peaked under **Suleyman I** (soo-lay-MAHN). By 1566 the Ottomans took control of the eastern Mediterranean and parts of Europe.

Meanwhile, the Safavids (sah-FAH-vuhds) gained power in the east. Before long, the Safavids came into conflict with the Ottomans and other Muslims. The conflict stemmed from an old disagreement about who should be caliph. In the mid-600s, Islam had split into two groups—the **Sunni** and the **Shia**. The Ottomans were Sunni, and the Safavids were Shia. The Safavid Empire conquered Persia in 1501.

East of the Safavid Empire, in India, lay the Mughal (MOO-guhl) Empire. The Mughals united many diverse peoples and were known for their architecture—particularly the Taj Mahal. Under the leader Akbar, the Mughal Empire was known for its religious tolerance. But more restrictive policies after his death led to the end of the empire.

> Underline the phrase that tells where the Ottomans found fierce soldiers to fight in their armies.

> What date signifies the absolute final end of the Roman Empire?
>
> _____
>
> _____

> Think of what you know about the Middle East today. Does the conflict between the Sunnis and the Shias continue?
>
> _____
>
> _____
>
> _____
>
> _____

CHALLENGE ACTIVITY

Critical Thinking: Drawing Inferences Draw a timeline marking the major Muslim conquests and a map to show the size of Islamic territory.

The Islamic World

MAIN IDEAS

1. Muslim scholars made lasting contributions to the fields of science and philosophy.

2. In literature and the arts, Muslim achievements included beautiful poetry, memorable short stories, and splendid architecture.

MAIN IDEAS

Key Terms and People

Ibn Battutah Muslim explorer and geographer

Sufism a movement of Islam, based on the belief that one must have a personal relationship with God

Omar Khayyám famous Sufi poet who wrote *The Rubáiyát*

patrons sponsors

minaret a narrow tower on a mosque from which Muslims are called to pray

calligraphy decorative writing

Section Summary

SCIENCE AND PHILOSOPHY

Islamic scholars made great advances in many fields. These included astronomy, geography, math, and science. At Baghdad and Córdoba, Greek and other writings were translated into Arabic. A common language helped scholars share research.

Muslim scientists built observatories to study the stars. They also improved the astrolabe. The Greeks had invented this tool to chart the position of the stars. The astrolabe would later be used in sea exploration.

It was a Muslim mathematician who invented algebra. Muslims found better ways to calculate distance and make precise maps. They also used the stars to navigate. Muslim merchants and explorers traveled wide and far. One great explorer was **Ibn Battutah**. He traveled to Africa, India, China, and Spain.

> Which two cities came to be recognized as the cultural capitals of Islam during the Middle Ages?
>
> _____
>
> _____
>
> _____

> Why do you think the astrolabe would be useful in sea exploration?
>
> _____
>
> _____
>
> _____

Muslims were also known in medicine. They added greatly to Greek and Indian medicine. Muslims also started the first school of pharmacy. A doctor in Baghdad found out how to detect and treat the disease smallpox. Another doctor, known in the West as Avicenna (av-uh-SEN-uh), wrote a medical encyclopedia. It was used widely in Europe for centuries.

A new philosophy developed. It was called **Sufism** (SOO-fi-zuhm). People who practice Sufism are Sufis (SOO-feez). Sufis seek a personal relationship with God. Sufism has brought many followers to Islam.

> **What two advances in medicine were made by Muslim doctors:**
> _____
> _____
> _____
> _____

LITERATURE AND THE ARTS

Poetry and short stories were popular among Muslims. The collection of stories called *The Thousand and One Nights* is still one of the best-loved books in the world. Sufi poets were popular, including the famous **Omar Khayyám** (OH-mahr ky-AHM).

> **What is the name of Islam's great collection of stories?**
> _____
> _____
> _____

There were many achievements in architecture. Rulers liked to be **patrons**. Patrons helped fund the design and construction of beautiful mosques. The main part of a mosque is a huge hall where thousands of people gather to pray. Often mosques have a large dome and a **minaret**.

Islam does not allow artists to show animals or humans in religious art. Muslims believe only Allah can create humans and animals or their images. In part for this reason, Muslim artists turned to **calligraphy**, This decorative writing became an art form.

> **Underline the sentence that helps to explain why Muslim artists developed calligraphy as a fine art**

CHALLENGE ACTIVITY

Critical Thinking: Drawing Inferences Islamic culture has created many advances in science, medicine, and art that we still use today. Pick the advance that you think is the most important to our modern society, and write a one-page paper explaining your position.

Early African Civilizations

CHAPTER SUMMARY

West African Timeline

c. 3000 BC	Climate changes as the desert expands; people settle in _____
c. 500 BC	West Africans learn how to make tools out of iron
c. 300 AD	Small bands of _____ defend themselves against _____
c. 800 AD	Ghana controls _____
c. 1200 AD	Ghana's decline caused by _____, _____, and _____
c. 1300 AD	In Mali, Mansa Musa establishes Timbuktu as a great center of Islamic culture
c. 1400s AD	_____ empire declines; _____ empire grows powerful under Sunni Ali
c. 1600 AD	_____ destroy Timbiktu and Gao; era of West African empires ends

COMPREHENSION AND CRITICAL THINKING

Use the answers to the following questions to fill in the graphic organizer above.

1. Explain When and why did West Africans first begin to settle in villages?

_____

2. Evaluate Why did West African society change dramatically in 300 AD?

_____

3. Identify Cause and Effect How did Ghana become the first West African empire? What were the causes of Ghana's decline?

_____

_____

4. Make Inferences In the 1400s, why did one empire gain power as another declined?

_____

_____

5. Identify Cause and Effect What led to the fall of the Songhai empire?

_____

Early African Civilizations

MAIN IDEAS

1. Landforms, climate, and resources affected the history of West Africa.
2. The way of life of early peoples in West Africa was shaped by family ties, religion, iron technology, and trade.

Key Terms and People

rifts long, deep valleys formed by movements of the earth's crust

sub-Saharan Africa Africa south of the Sahara Desert

Sahel a strip of land in West Africa that divides the desert from wetter areas

savannah open grassland with scattered trees

rain forests dense, wet forests near the equator

extended family parents, children, and near relatives who all live in one household

animism the belief that bodies of water, animals, trees and other natural objects have spirits

Section Summary

LANDFORMS, CLIMATE, AND RESOURCES

Africa is the second-largest continent in the world. The Sahara Desert stretches across North Africa. There are also mighty mountain chains. In eastern Africa, mountains extend along **rifts**. These are long, deep valleys formed by movements of the earth's crust. There are large rivers that cross the plains of **sub-Saharan Africa**.

> **What caused the great rift valleys of eastern Africa?**
> _____
> _____
> _____

Great civilizations grew up along the Niger River. The Niger River's middle section has several low-lying lakes and marshes. Many animals and plants flourish in this area.

Four different regions make up the area around the Niger. The regions, running from east to west, range from very dry and sandy to very wet and green. The northern band is the southern part of the Sahara desert, so it is hot and dry here. Next is the **Sahel**, a strip of land that divides the desert from the wetter areas. Then there is the **savannah**,

> **What are the four regions around the Niger River?**
> _____
> _____
> _____
> _____

which has open grasslands. The fourth region is **rain forest** a dense, wet area with lots of trees and plants. The rain forests lie near the equator.

West Africa's farm land is a major resource. Its different climates help grow many different types of crops. These crops include dates from the desert and medicinal kola nuts from the forest. Minerals such as gold and salt are also an important resource.

What two areas along the Niger are good for grazing cattle?

_____
_____
_____

EARLY PEOPLE'S WAY OF LIFE

A typical West African family was an **extended family**. In an extended family, parents, children, and near relatives all live in one household. In some areas, men or women born within two to three years of each other formed age-sets.

Can you name another group who value the extended family?

_____
_____

Loyalty to family and age-sets helped support village life. The men hunted and farmed. The women took care of the children, farmed, gathered firewood, carried water, and ground grain.

Religion was also central to West African life. Most villagers believed that the spirits of their ancestors stayed close by to their village. They set up statues in honor of their dead ancestors. Another common belief was **animism**, the belief that animals, trees, bodies of water, and other natural objects have spirits.

Explain very briefly how the family is central even to West African religion.

_____
_____
_____
_____
_____

Over time new discoveries changed West African culture. Around 500 BC, West Africans learned how to make tools out of iron. With iron tools, people could cut down trees and make more land useable for farming. With more resources, the people had surpluses that they could trade. They traded gold, salt, cloth, and human slaves. Traders crossed the Sahara to North Africa and the Islamic world.

CHALLENGE ACTIVITY

Critical Thinking: Drawing Inferences Early West African culture might seem very different from our modern world. Are there any similarities between the ways the early West Africans lived and the way you live? Write a one-page essay explaining your answer.

Early African Civilizations

> **MAIN IDEAS**
> 1. Ghana controlled trade and became wealthy.
> 2. Through its control of trade, Ghana built an empire.
> 3. Ghana's decline was caused by attacking invaders, overgrazing, and the loss of trade.

Key Terms and People

silent barter a process in which people exchange goods without ever contacting each other directly

Tunka Manin Ghana's king who ruled the empire at the height of its power

Academic Vocabulary

process a series of steps by which a task is accomplished

Section Summary

GHANA CONTROLS TRADE

Ghana (GAH-nuh) was the first West African empire to profit from Saharan trade by controlling trade routes. Ghana lay between the Niger and Senegal rivers in sub-Saharan Africa, northwest of the nation now called Ghana.

Historians think the first people in Ghana were farmers. Starting around 300, these farmers were threatened by nomadic herders. The herders wanted the water and pastures. For protection, small groups began to band together. These groups grew stronger with the introduction of farming tools and weapons made of iron.

Ghana's territory lay between the desert and the forests. These were areas rich with salt and gold. The gold and salt trade sometimes followed a **process** called **silent barter**. In this process people exchange goods without contacting each other directly. This ensured peaceful business and kept the location of the gold mines secret.

> **What economic factor was Ghana the first in West Africa to exploit?**
> _____
> _____

> **Which was more valuable, salt or gold? Why?**
> _____
> _____
> _____
> _____

As populations grew and trade increased, the rulers of Ghana grew stronger. Their armies used iron weapons. They took control of the trade routes that had been run by North African merchants.

GHANA BUILDS AN EMPIRE

By 800, Ghana was firmly in control of West Africa's trade routes. As a result, trade became safer and Ghana's influence increased. Traders were charged a tax to enter or leave Ghana. The kings made it illegal for anyone other than themselves to own gold. They also taxed the people of Ghana.

The kings increased the size of Ghana by conquering other tribes. However, Ghana's kings allowed former rulers to keep much of their own power. These kings acted as governors of their territories. The empire of Ghana reached its peak under **Tunka Manin** (TOOHN-kah MAH-nin).

> When the kings made it illegal for anyone else to own gold, what happened to the value of gold? Explain.
>
> _____
>
> _____

GHANA'S DECLINE

By the early 1200s, Ghana had collapsed. Three major factors contributed to its decline. A group of Muslim Berbers called the Almoravids invaded and weakened the empire. These Berbers were herders. Their animals overgrazed and ruined the farmland. Many farmers left. At the same time, internal rebellions led to Ghana's loss of control over trade routes.

> List two reasons for the decline of Ghana's empire.
>
> _____
>
> _____
>
> _____

CHALLENGE ACTIVITY

Critical Thinking: Drawing Inferences Recreate the silent barter system in the classroom. Divide students into groups of gold and salt traders. Each group of "traders" should write a one-page paper detailing the advantages and disadvantages of silent barter.

Early African Civilizations

MAIN IDEAS

1. The empire of Mali reached its height under the ruler Mansa Musa, but the empire fell to invaders in the 1400s.
2. The Songhai built a new Islamic empire in West Africa, conquering many of the lands that were once part of Mali.
3. Great Zimbabwe was a powerful state that developed in southern Africa.

Key Terms and People

Sundiata ruler that led the Mali Empire's rise to power

Mansa Musa Muslim king who ruled the Mali Empire at the height of its power and spread Islam through a large part of Africa

Sunni Ali first leader of Songhai, the last of the great West African empires

Askia the Great Muslim ruler who led Songhai to the height of its power

Section Summary

MALI

Like Ghana, Mali (MAH-lee) lays along the upper Niger River. Mali's location on the Niger River allowed its people to control trade on the river. Mali's rise to power began under a ruler named **Sundiata** (soohn-JAHT-ah).

A cruel ruler conquered Mali when Sundiata was a boy. When Sundiata grew older, he raised an army and won Mali's independence. Sundiata conquered nearby kingdoms, including Ghana, and took over the salt and gold trades. He also took over religious and political authority held by local leaders.

Mali's greatest and most famous ruler was a Muslim named **Mansa Musa** (MAHN-sah moo-SAH). Under his leadership, Mali reached its peak. Musa ruled Mali for about 25 years and captured many important trading cities. He also made the Islamic world aware of Mali on his pilgrimage to Mecca.

Mansa Musa stressed the importance of learning Arabic in order to read the Qur'an. He spread Islam through West Africa by building mosques in cities.

> **What river flowed through both Ghana and Mali?**
> _____
> _____

> **Name three important things Mansa Musa did as leader of Mali.**
> _____
> _____
> _____

Interactive Reader and Study Guide

After Mansa Musa died, invaders destroyed the schools and mosques of Timbuktu. Rebel groups seized the city. By 1500 nearly all of the lands the empire had once ruled were lost.

SONGHAI

As Mali declined, a people called the Songhai (SAHNG-hy) grew in strength. In the 1300s, the Songhai lands lay within the empire of Mali. As Mali weakened, the Songhai broke free. Songhai leader **Sunni Ali** (SOOH-nee ah-LEE) strengthened and enlarged the Songhai empire.

After Sunni Ali died, his son Sunni Baru became ruler. He was not Muslim. But most of the people of the empire's towns were Muslim. They feared that if Sunni Baru did not support Islam they would lose trade and power, so they rebelled. After overthrowing Sunni Baru, the leader of that rebellion became known as **Askia the Great**.

Muslim culture and education thrived during Askia's reign. Timbuktu's universities, schools, libraries, and mosques attracted thousands.

Morocco invaded Songhai and destroyed Gao and Timbuktu. Songhai never recovered and trade declined. Other trade centers north and south of the old empire became more important. The period of great West African empires came to an end.

> **Why was Sunni Baru overthrown?**
> _____
> _____
> _____
> _____

> **Do research on the Internet or in a library and find the population of Timbuktu today. Write that figure here:**
> _____
> _____

GREAT ZIMBABWE

In southern Africa, a great kingdom arose in the late 1000s called Great Zimbabwe. Farming, gold mining, and trading made the rulers wealthy and powerful. But in the 1400s, the gold trade declined, and by 1500, Great Zimbabwe was no longer a political and trading center.

CHALLENGE ACTIVITY

Critical Thinking: Drawing Inferences You are reporter who does not know much about Africa. One day, the ruler of Mali or Songhai comes through your city. Write an article about this person.

Early African Civilizations

> **MAIN IDEAS**
> 1. West Africans have preserved their history through storytelling and the written accounts of visitors.
> 2. Through art, music, and dance, West Africans have expressed their creativity and kept alive their cultural traditions.

Key Terms and People

oral history a spoken record of past events

griots West African storytellers responsible for reciting oral history

proverbs short sayings of wisdom or truth

kente handwoven, brightly colored cloth made in West Africa

Section Summary

PRESERVING HISTORY

Although cities like Timbuktu and Djenné were known for their universities and libraries, writing was not common in West Africa. None of the major early civilizations of West Africa developed a written language. Arabic was the only written language used. Instead of writing their history, West Africans passed along information about their civilization through **oral history** in their native languages.

The task of remembering and telling West Africa's history was entrusted to storytellers called **griots** (GREE-ohz). Griots tried to make their stories entertaining. They also told **proverbs,** or short sayings of wisdom or truth. The griots had to memorize hundreds of names and dates. Some griots confused names and events in their heads, so some stories might became distorted. Still, much knowledge could be gained by listening to a griot.

The histories of empires were often told as epic poems, long poems about kingdoms and heroes. Many of these poems were collected in the *Dausi* (DAW-zee) and the *Sundiata.* The *Dausi* tells the history of Ghana, but it also includes myths and

> **Did Arabic replace the native languages of the West Africans? How do you know your answer is correct?**
>
> _____
> _____
> _____
> _____

> **Why might the history of the griots not be perfectly accurate?**
>
> _____
> _____
> _____
> _____

legends. The *Sundiata* tells the story of Mali's first ruler. A conqueror killed his family, but the boy was spared because he was sick. He grew up to be a great warrior and overthrew the conqueror.

Though the West Africans left no written histories, visitors from other parts of the world did write about the region. Much of what we know about early West Africa comes from the writings of travelers and scholars from Muslim lands such as Spain and Arabia. Ibn Battutah was the most famous visitor to write about West Africa.

ART, MUSIC, AND DANCE

Besides storytelling, West African cultures considered other art forms, including sculpture, mask-making, cloth-making, music, and dance just as important. West African artists made sculptures of people from wood, brass, clay, ivory, stone, and other materials. Some of these images have inspired modern artists like Matisse and Picasso.

> Circle the names of the modern artists inspired by the images crafted by West African sculptors.

West Africans are also known for distinctive mask-making and textiles. Particularly prized is the brightly colored **kente** (ken-TAY), a hand-woven cloth that was worn by kings and queens on special occasions.

In many West African societies, music and dance were as important as the visual arts. Singing, dancing, and drumming were great entertainment, but they also helped people celebrate their history and were central to many religious celebrations.

> List three ways in which music had a place in West African culture.
>
> _____
> _____
> _____
> _____

CHALLENGE ACTIVITY

Critical Thinking: Drawing Inferences Much of what we know about West Africa comes from oral traditions or accounts by visitors to the land. Write one page evaluating the accuracy of these resources. Which sources are primary, which are secondary? Consider how much a visitor who was not raised in a culture can really understand about that culture.

China

CHAPTER SUMMARY

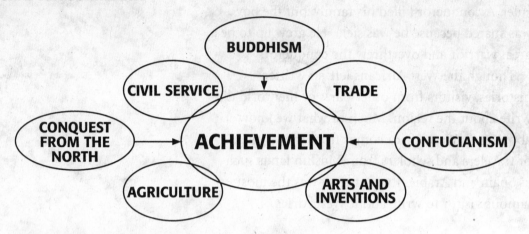

COMPREHENSION AND CRITICAL THINKING

Use information from the graphic organizer to answer the following questions.

1. **Identify** From which direction did invaders of China almost always come?

_____

_____

2. **Draw inference** Confucianism emphasized order in society. Which category of achievement do you think was most influenced by Confucianism?

_____

_____

3. **Evaluate** Why do you think agricultural achievements such as irrigation and faster-growing crops lead to increased trade?

_____

_____

4. **Recall** What major world religion exerted a powerful influence on Chinese culture?

_____

_____

China

Section 1

MAIN IDEAS
1. The Period of Disunion was a time of war and disorder that followed the end of the Han dynasty.
2. China was reunified under the Sui, Tang, and Song dynasties.
3. The Age of Buddhism saw major religious changes in China.

Key Terms and People

Empress Wu Tang ruler whose methods were sometimes vicious, but whose reign was stable and prosperous

Section Summary

THE PERIOD OF DISUNION

After the Han dynasty collapsed in 220, China was split into several competing kingdoms, each ruled by military leaders. This time is called the Period of Disunion. The era lasted for more than 350 years, from 220 to 589. During this period, nomadic tribes settled in northern China, and many northern Chinese moved south. These movements resulted in blended cultures in both north and south China.

> **What were the two general elements in the blended culture of northern China during the Period of Disunion?**
> _____
> _____
> _____

THE SUI, TANG, AND SONG

After this time of political confusion and cultural change, China was reunified. Under the Sui, Tang, and Song dynasties, China remained unified for most of the next 700 years.

The Sui (SWAY) dynasty was established by a northern leader called Yang Chien (YANG jee-en). In 589 he led his army to conquer lands to the west and south and reunified China. The Tang dynasty replaced the Sui in 618. The Tang ruled China for nearly 300 years. During this period, Chinese power and influence reached all of east and Southeast Asia, as well as much of Central Asia.

> **Who was the first Sui ruler?**
> _____
> _____

> **How many years did the Sui dynasty last?**
> _____
> _____

Historians view the Tang dynasty as a golden age of Chinese civilization. Among its leaders, three are especially notable. Taizong (TY-tzoong) conquered most of Central Asia, reformed the military, and created law codes. In the reign of Xuanzong (SHOO-AN-tzoong), culture flourished and many of China's finest poets wrote. **Empress Wu**, the only woman to rule China, ruled with an iron first, but she but kept China stable and prosperous.

After the Tang dynasty fell, China entered a period of 53 years known as Five Dynasties and Ten Kingdoms. Then, in 960, China was again reunified under the Song dynasty, and another great period of accomplishment began that lasted for about 300 years, until 1279.

> **Name three important Tang rulers.**
> _____
> _____
> _____

THE AGE OF BUDDHISM

During the troubled Period of Disunion, many Chinese people turned to Buddhism. They took comfort in the Buddhist teaching that people can escape suffering and achieve a state of peace. During the Sui and Tang dynasties, Buddhism became well established throughout China and Buddhist temples arose across the land.

Buddhism influenced many aspects of Chinese culture, including art, literature, and architecture. Chinese Buddhist missionaries brought the religion to Japan, Korea, and other Asian lands. Despite a Tang emperor's campaign against the religion, Buddhism remained a vital part of Chinese culture.

> **Why do you think Buddhism comforted people during the Period of Disunion?**
> _____
> _____
> _____
> _____

CHALLENGE ACTIVITY

Critical Thinking: Sequence Research the origin and development of Buddhism before it became popular in China.

China

MAIN IDEAS
1. Advances in agriculture led to increased trade and population growth.
2. Cities and trade grew during the Tang and Song dynasties
3. The Tang and Song dynasties produced fine arts and inventions.

Key Terms and People

porcelain a thin, beautiful pottery invented by the Chinese

gunpowder a mixture of powders used in guns and explosives

compass an instrument that uses the earth's magnetic field to indicate direction

woodblock printing a form of printing in which an entire page is carved into a block of wood that is covered with ink and then pressed against paper to make a copy of the page

Section Summary

ADVANCES IN AGRICULTURE

Under the Song dynasty, Chinese agriculture reached new heights. Farmers created elaborate irrigation systems based on new techniques and devices. The amount of land under cultivation increased. Farmers developed a new type of fast-ripening rice that enabled them to grow two or even three crops in the time it used to take to grow just one. They also learned to grow cotton efficently and processed the fiber to make clothes and other goods.

Merchants traded food crops, so food was abundant not just in the countryside but in the cities, too. Population grew to more than 100 million people, making China the most populous country in the world.

What was the advantage of fast-ripening rice?

_____

_____

_____

Do you think agricultural abundance and the growth of cities are connected? Why?

_____

_____

_____

_____

CITIES AND TRADE

Chinese cities grew and flourished as the trade centers of the Tang and Song dynasties. Chang'an (chahng-AHN), with a population of more than a million people, was by far the largest city in the world at the time. Traders used the Grand Canal, a series of waterways that linked major cities, to ship goods and agricultural products throughout China.

Foreign trade used both land routes and sea routes. China's Pacific ports were open to foreign traders. A bustling trade was carried on with India, Africa, and Southwest Asia. Chinese exports included tea, rice, spices, and jade. Especially prized by foreigners, however, were silk and **porcelain**. The methods of making these Chinese inventions were kept secret for centuries.

> **Why do you think the Chinese did not want foreigners to know how to make silk and porcelain?**
> _____
> _____
> _____
> _____

ARTS AND INVENTIONS

The Tang dynasty produced some of China's greatest artists and writers, including Li Po and Du Fu—the most famous of all Chinese poets—and the Buddhist painter Wu Daozi (DOW-tzee). The Song dynasty produced Li Qingzhao (ching-ZHOW), perhaps China's greatest female poet. Artists of both dynasties created exquisite objects in clay, particularly porcelain items with a pale green glaze called celadon (SEL-uh-duhn).

> **Use the Internet or a library to find a poem by Li Po.**

The Tang and Song dynasties produced some of the most remarkable—and important—inventions in human history, including **gunpowder** and the **compass**.

The world's oldest-known printed book, using **woodblock printing**, was printed in China in 868. Later, during the Song dynasty, the Chinese invented movable type for printing. The Song dynasty also introduced the concept of paper money.

> **What printing technology ultimately superseded woodblock printing?**
> _____
> _____

CHALLENGE ACTIVITY

Critical Thinking: Drawing Inferences Create a document showing an exchange of goods between a Song dynasty Chinese trader and a foreign merchant.

China

Section 3

MAIN IDEAS

1. Confucianism underwent changes and influenced Chinese government.
2. Scholar-officials ran China's government during the Song dynasty.

Key Terms and People

bureaucracy body of unelected government officials

civil service service as a government official

scholar-official an educated member of the government

Academic Vocabulary

function work or perform

incentive something that leads people to follow a certain course of action

Section Summary

CONFUCIANISM

Confucianism is the name given to the ideas of the Chinese philosopher Confucius. Confucius's teachings focused on ethics, or proper behavior, of individuals and governments. He argued that society would **function** best if everyone followed two principles, *ren* and *li*. *Ren* means concern for others, and *li* means following appropriate customs and behavior. Order in society is maintained when people know their place and behave appropriately.

> Conduct some research to find the title usually given in English to a book containing Confucius's ideas. Write that title here.
>
> _____
> _____

For a thousand years after his death, Confucius's ideas went in and out of favor several times. Early in the Song dynasty, however, a new version of Confucianism, known as neo-Confucianism, was adopted as official government policy. In addition to teaching proper behavior, neo-Confucian scholars and officials discussed spiritual questions like what made human beings do bad things even if their basic nature was good.

> Before the Song dynasty, what religious belief probably had a negative effect on the popularity of Confucianism in China?
>
> _____
> _____

SCHOLAR-OFFICIALS

The Song dynasty took another major step that would affect the Chinese imperial state for centuries to come. The Song established a system by which people went to work for the government. These workers formed a large **bureaucracy** by passing a series of written **civil service** examinations.

> **Name a well-known government today that has a large bureaucracy.**
> _____
> _____

The tests covered both the traditional teachings of Confucius and spiritual questions. Because the tests were extremely difficult, students spent years preparing for them. Often only very few students passed the exam. Candidates had a strong **incentive** for studying hard. Passing the tests meant life as a **scholar-official**, whose benefits included considerable respect, a good salary, and reduced penalties for breaking the law.

> **Draw a picture of what you think a Song scholar-official might look like.**

The civil service examination system helped ensure that talented, intelligent people became scholar-officials. This system was a major factor in the stability of the Song government.

CHALLENGE ACTIVITY

Critical Thinking: Drawing Inferences Write a short essay on the relation between the Song dynasty development of civil service and the Confucian ideals of *ren* and *li*.

Interactive Reader and Study Guide

China

Section 4

MAIN IDEAS

1. The Mongol Empire included China, and the Mongols ruled China as the Yuan dynasty.
2. The Ming dynasty was a time of stability and prosperity.
3. China under the Ming saw great changes in its government and relations with other countries.

Key Terms and People

Genghis Khan powerful leader who united the Mongols

Kublai Khan Genghis Khan's grandson, who completed the conquest of China

Zheng He famous seafaring voyager of the Ming dynasty

isolationism a policy of removing a country from contact with other countries

Academic Vocabulary

consequences effects of a particular event or events

Section Summary

THE MONGOL EMPIRE

For centuries, the Mongols had lived as nomadic tribes in the vast plains north of China. Then in 1206, a powerful leader known as **Genghis Khan** (jeng-giz KAHN) united them. He led huge armies on bloody expeditions of conquest throughout much of Asia and Eastern Europe.

Genghis Khan first led his armies into northern China in 1211. They fought their way south, wrecking whole towns and ruining farmland. By the time of Genghis Khan's death in 1227, all of northern China was under Mongol control.

Genghis Khan's grandson, **Kublai Khan** (KOO-bluh KAHN), completed the conquest of China and declared himself emperor of China in 1279. He named his new dynasty the Yuan dynasty. Kublai

> What country today represents the homeland of the Mongols?
>
> _____
>
> _____

> How many years did it take for the Mongol armies to conquer all of China?
>
> _____
>
> _____

Khan's empire, which stretched all the way to eastern Europe, covered more land than any other empire in world history.

Kublai Khan's regime preserved much of the structure of the Song dynasty, including the civil service and trade routes. The Italian merchant Marco Polo, who traveled in China between 1271 and 1295, wrote of a highly civilized country and sparked Europeans' interest in China.

Two failed campaigns against Japan and expensive public works projects gradually weakened the Yuan dynasty. Many Chinese groups rebelled. Finally, in 1368, Chu Yuan-Chang (JOO yoo-ahn-JAHNG) took control and founded the Ming dynasty.

> Which two aspects of Song civilization would you say Kublai Khan appreciated the most?
> _____
> _____
> _____

THE MING DYNASTY

The Ming dynasty lasted nearly 300 years, from 1368 to 1644. Ming China proved to be one of the most stable and prosperous times in Chinese history. Great Ming achievements include the fabulous ships and goodwill voyages of **Zheng He** (juhng HUH), the famous Forbidden City at the center of Beijing, and the Great Wall of China.

> What do you think was the original reason for building the Great Wall?
> _____
> _____
> _____
> _____

CHINA UNDER THE MING

Around 1400 China's emperor and scholar-officials began to react against the popular influence of foreign goods, beliefs, and customs, and the increasing wealth and power of merchants. China entered a period of **isolationism**. Ironically, the **consequences** of this policy included a weakness that allowed opportunistic Westerners to seize considerable power in some parts of China as China's imperial glory faded.

> Name another major country whose history includes a period of isolationism.
> _____
> _____

CHALLENGE ACTIVITY

Critical Thinking: Drawing Inferences Draw a street map of an imaginary city. Include a "forbidden city" within it that is restricted to a certain group of your choosing.

Japan

CHAPTER SUMMARY

Cause	→	Effect
	→	The first Japanese rulers
Prince Shotoku's reign	→	
The emperor's move to Heian court	→	Daimyos hiring shoguns and samurai for protection

COMPREHENSION AND CRITICAL THINKING

Use the answers to the following questions to fill in the graphic organizer above.

1. Explain Who were the first rulers of Japan and how did they get to be rulers?

_____

_____

2. Identify Cause and Effect How did Prince Shotoku's interest in all things Chinese impact Japanese culture?

_____

_____

3. Evaluate Why were the Japanese willing to submit to shogun and samurai rule?

_____

_____

4. Draw a Conclusion Why do you think the shogun kept the emperor in place as a figurehead, even though the emperor was a ruler with no power?

_____

_____

Japan

Section 1

MAIN IDEAS

1. Geography shaped life in Japan.
2. Early Japanese society was organized in clans, which came to be ruled by an emperor.
3. Japan learned about language, society, and government from China and Korea.

Key Terms and People

clans extended families

Shinto the traditional religion of Japan, based on the belief that everything in nature has a spirit

Prince Shotoku popular Japanese ruler who brought many Chinese ideas to Japan

regent someone who rules for someone who is unable rule alone

Section Summary

GEOGRAPHY SHAPES LIFE IN JAPAN

The islands of Japan are the tops of undersea mountains and volcanoes. Because it is difficult to live and farm on mountain slopes, most Japanese people have always lived in the few flat areas along the coastal plains.

The nearness of the sea means that seafood has been a key part of the Japanese diet for thousands of years. Isolation has contributed to a distinctive Japanese culture, although the Japanese have been influenced by nearby Korea and China.

> Why is most of Japan's land hilly, and not flat?
>
> _____
> _____
> _____
> _____

EARLY JAPANESE SOCIETY

Early Japan was home to two different cultures, neither of which had much—if any—contact with the rest of Asia. The Ainu (EYE-noo), with a look and language distinct from the rest of Asia, were driven by conflict to the northern island of Hokkaido. Over time, the Ainu culture almost disappeared.

> What geographic feature is probably the main reason why Japan's early culture was so distinct from that of other parts of Asia?
>
> _____
> _____
> _____

The people living to the south of the Ainu eventually became the Japanese. They lived mostly in small farm villages. **Clans**, or extended families, ruled these villages. They practiced religious rituals that became **Shinto**, the traditional religion of Japan. According to this tradition, everything in nature has a spirit, or *kami* (KAH-mee).

Some clans became so powerful that they took over much of Japan. The Yamato rulers were the first clan to call themselves emperors of Japan.

> **What was the unit of political life in early Japan?**
> _____
> _____

JAPAN LEARNS FROM CHINA AND KOREA

By the mid-500s, Japanese rulers yearned to learn new things. They sent emissaries to Korea and China to learn about those cultures. Chinese culture was very influential in Japan. With no written language of their own, the Japanese used Chinese characters to spell out Japanese sounds and words. Chinese was actually Japan's official language from about 500 to about 1100.

> **For about how many centuries was Chinese the official language of Japan?**
> _____
> _____

Prince Shotoku (shoh-toh-koo), who served as **regent** for his aunt the empress, was a major proponent of Chinese culture. Shotoku had advisors introduce the Chinese philosophy of Confucianism to Japan. He also encouraged the spread of Buddhism. Shotoku's attempt to bring a more absolute, Chinese-style of rule to Japan did not fare as well. Clan leaders opposed it. They were afraid to give up their power. Prince Shotoku died without achieving his goals. Later rulers put many of his ideas in practice, though.

> **Underline the sentence that explains why the clan leaders did not want a Chinese-style rule.**

CHALLENGE ACTIVITY

Critical Thinking: Drawing Inferences Why do you think the Japanese were so interested in learning from the Chinese and the Koreans? Write a one-page essay describing specific examples of what China and other cultures offered that Japan did not have at the time.

Japan

MAIN IDEAS

1. Japanese nobles created great art in their court at Heian.
2. Buddhism changed in Japan during the Heian period.

Key Terms and People

court group of nobles who serve as advisors to a ruler

Lady Murasaki Shikibu Japanese writer credited with writing the world's first novel

Zen form of Buddhism involving quiet, thoughtful meditation

Section Summary

JAPANESE NOBLES CREATE GREAT ART

In 794 the emperor and empress of Japan moved to Heian (HAY-ahn), a city now called Kyoto. The nobles who followed created an imperial **court**. These nobles had little to do with the common people of Heian. They lived apart from poorer citizens and seldom left the city. They loved beauty and made the court at Heian the center of a golden age of art and learning between 794 and 1185.

These nobles dressed in beautiful silk robes and carried decorative fans. They were also lovers of the written and spoken word, and spent many hours writing in journals. Several women of the Heian court wrote in the Japanese language, although Chinese was the official language. As a result, women wrote most of the major works of early Japanese literature.

Probably the greatest of these early writers was **Lady Murasaki Shikibu** (moohr-ah-sahk-ee shee-kee-boo). Around 1000, she wrote *The Tale of Genji*, often considered the world's first full-length novel. It is the story of a prince named Genji and his quest for love. During his search he meets women from many different social classes.

> Why do you think the nobles of Heian devoted so much time to the promotion of the arts?
>
> _____
> _____
> _____
> _____

> Circle the name of the author of what is considered the world's first novel.

Visual arts were also popular, particularly painting, calligraphy, and architecture. The paintings were made in bright, bold colors. Most Heian architecture was based on that of the Chinese capital. Other architectural styles were simple and airy. Wood houses with tiled roofs featured large open spaces surrounded by elegant gardens. Performing arts also flourished at the Heian court, particularly a form of drama called Noh, which combined music, dance and speaking parts. Noh plays often presented the feats of great Japanese heroes.

> **What class of people do you think provided food and services for the Heian court?**
> _____
> _____

BUDDHISM CHANGES

Common Japanese people had no time for the long, elaborate rituals practiced by the court. Both groups were deeply religious, however. The Japanese introduced important changes to the Buddhism, which had been brought from China. Some new forms of Buddhism blended elements of Shinto Other forms were unique to Japan. One very popular form, called Pure Land Buddhism, did not require any special rituals. Instead, Pure Land Buddhists chanted the Buddha's name over and over again.

> **What did Pure Land Buddhism require of its followers?**
> _____
> _____
> _____

In the 1100s a new form of Buddhism called **Zen** developed. Zen Buddhists believed that neither faith nor good behavior led to wisdom. Instead, people should practice self-discipline and meditation, or quiet thinking. These ideas appealed to many Japanese, especially warriors. As these warriors gained more influence in Japan, so did Zen Buddhism.

> **Underline the phrase that defines the central practices of Zen Buddhism.**

CHALLENGE ACTIVITY

Critical Thinking: Drawing Inferences If you were a noble in the Heian court who did not have to work, what would you do all day? Write a journal entry in the style and manner of a Japanese noble, describing a typical day.

Japan

MAIN IDEAS

1. Samurai and shoguns took over Japan as emperors lost influence.
2. Samurai warriors lived honorably.
3. Order broke down when the power of the shoguns was challenged by invaders and rebellions.
4. Strong leaders took over and reunified Japan.

Key Terms and People

daimyo large landowner

samurai trained professional warriors

figurehead a person who appears to rule though real power rests with someone else

shogun a general who ruled Japan in the emperor's name

Bushido the strict samurai code of rules

Section Summary

SAMURAI AND SHOGUNS TAKE OVER JAPAN

While the Heian court flourished, order was breaking down in Japanese society. By the late 1100s, powerful nobles were openly at war. Rebels fought against imperial officials. Japan's rulers did not notice the problems growing in their country.

Japan's large landowners, or **daimyo** (DY-mee-oh), decided they could not rely on the emperor to protect them. They hired **samurai** (SA-muh-ry), trained professional warriors, to defend their property. Several noble clans decided to seize power themselves.

> Underline the phrase that explains why the daimyo went out and hired their own protection in the late 1100s.

Two of these clans fought each other fiercely for 30 years. Finally, the head of the Minamoto clan declared himself Japan's new ruler. The Minamoto leader kept the emperor on as a **figurehead**. The Minamoto leader took the title **shogun**. He ruled in

> To what clan did Japan's first shogun belong?
>
> _____
>
> _____

Interactive Reader and Study Guide

the emperor's name. When he died, he passed his title and power on to one of his children. For about the next 700 years, Japan was ruled by shoguns.

> Circle how many years the shoguns would rule Japan.

SAMURAI LIVE HONORABLY

The samurai enjoyed many privileges, but also had to follow a strict code of rules called **Bushido** (booh-shi-doh). Loyalty and honor were central to this code. Both men and women of samurai families learned to fight.

ORDER BREAKS DOWN

The shoguns, with the help of the samurai, kept order in Japan for nearly a century. Slowly that order broke down. Two foreign invasions by the Mongols were stopped, but the authority of the shoguns weakened. Increasingly, nobles began to resent the shoguns' power over them. The daimyo and the emperor worked together to limit the power of the shogun.

> Why do you think the emperor might resent the power of the shoguns?
>
> _____
> _____
> _____
> _____

STRONG LEADERS TAKE OVER

Eventually, new leaders rose to power. Each fought to unify all of Japan under his control. The first to restore the power of the shogun was Oda Nobunaga (ohd-ah noh-booh-nah-gah), who ruled half of Japan by 1582. Other shoguns who followed stabilized Japanese rule. The shogun Tokugawa Ieyasu (toh-koohg-ah-wuh ee-e-yahs-ooh) sent emissaries out to the world. Others, however, feared the intrusion of foreigners. In 1630, the reigning shogun closed off Japan completely. This extended the samurai period until the 1800s.

> Which shogun opened Japan up the world?
>
> _____
> _____

CHALLENGE ACTIVITY

Critical Thinking: Drawing Inferences You are an ordinary Japanese citizen living in the Middle Ages. To whom do you pledge the highest allegiance—the gods, the emperor, the shogun, or the samurai who work for them? Explain your reasoning in a one-page essay.

The Early Americas

CHAPTER SUMMARY

Comparing the Maya, Aztec, and Inca

	Maya	Aztec	Inca
Taxes		Tributes of cotton, gold, or food	Labor
Upper Classes	King, priests, warriors, merchants	King, nobles, priests, warriors	
Lower Classes	Farmers	Farmers and laborers; slaves	
Language	Writing		No writing
Sacrifices	Blood, human sacrifice		Llamas, cloth, or food
Structures		Temples, palace, causeways	Massive stones in buildings, network of roads
Condition of Empire when Spanish Arrived	Civilization in decline	Empire at peak	

COMPREHENSION AND CRITICAL THINKING

Use the answers to the following questions to fill in the graphic organizer above.

1. Contrast In what form were taxes collected in each civilization?

_____

_____

2. Compare and Contrast Name at least two differences and two similarities among the Maya, Aztec, and Inca civilizations.

_____

_____

3. Draw a Conclusion Although they were greatly outnumbered, Spanish conquistadors conquered all three empires. Explain how this was possible.

_____

_____

_____

Section 1

> **MAIN IDEAS**
> 1. Geography affected the life of the early Maya in Mesoamerica.
> 2. During the Classic Age, the Maya built great cities linked by trade.
> 3. Maya culture was influenced by social structure, religion, and achievements in science and the arts.
> 4. The decline of Maya civilization began in the 900s, for reasons that are still unclear.

Key Terms and People

maize corn

observatories buildings designed to study astronomy and view the stars

Academic Vocabulary

aspect a part of something

rebel to fight against authority

Section Summary

GEOGRAPHY AND THE EARLY MAYA

Mesoamerica extends from the middle Mexico to Central America. The Maya (MY-uh) civilization developed here around 1000 BC. Thick forests covered the area, so the Maya had cleared the area to farm. They grew **maize**, or corn, and beans, squash, and avocados. The forest was also a source of many resources, including animals for food and wood for building materials. The Maya lived in villages. By AD 200, the Maya were building large cities.

> Underline the description of the land included in the area called Mesoamerica.

THE CLASSIC AGE

Maya civilization was at its peak between AD 250 and 900, a period called the Classic Age. There were more than more than 40 Maya city-states. They traded crops, wood, jade, and obsidian.

The Maya built large stone pyramids, temples, and palaces. Some buildings honored local kings. A temple built in the city of Palenque (pah-LENG-kay)

> List three valued Maya exports.
> _____
> _____
> _____
> _____

Interactive Reader and Study Guide

honored the king Pacal (puh-KAHL). The Maya built canals to bring water to the cities. They also shaped hillsides into flat terraces for crops.

> **How do historians know about the rule of the Maya king Pacal?**
> _____
> _____
> _____
> _____

MAYA CULTURE

The Maya had a complex social structure. Kings held the highest position. Priests, warriors, and merchants made up the upper class. Most Maya belonged to lower class farming families. Maya farmers had to "pay" the rulers with some of their crops and with goods such as cloth and salt. They also had to help build temples and other buildings.

The Maya worshipped many gods. Each god represented a different **aspect** of life. The Maya tried to keep the gods happy by giving them blood.

> **What did the Maya think their gods wanted in order to be appeased?**
> _____
> _____

Maya achievements in art, architecture, math, science, and writing were remarkable. They built **observatories** for priests to study the stars. They learned that the year had about 365 days. The Maya developed a complex number system and a writing system. They also made jade and gold jewelry.

DECLINE OF MAYA CIVILIZATION

Maya civilization began to collapse in the 900s. They stopped building large buildings and left the cities for the countryside. Historians are not sure why this happened, but there are several theories.

Some historians believe that Maya farmers kept planting the same crop over and over, which weakened the soil. This may have caused more competition and war between the cities. The people may have decided to **rebel** against their kings' demands. There probably were many factors that led to the decline of the Maya civilization.

> **List two factors that may have contributed to the decline of the Maya civilization.**
> _____
> _____
> _____

CHALLENGE ACTIVITY

Critical Thinking: Drawing Inferences One source of information about the Maya comes from kings like Pacal, who dedicated a temple to his achievements. Draw a building that honors our culture. Include details that would help future historians reconstruct 21st century life.

The Early Americas

> **MAIN IDEAS**
> 1. The Aztecs built a rich and powerful empire in central Mexico.
> 2. Life in the empire was shaped by social structure, religion, and warfare.
> 3. Hernán Cortés conquered the Aztec Empire in 1521.

Key Terms and People

causeways raised paths across water or wet ground

Hernán Cortés Spanish conquistador leader who conquered the Aztec Empire

conquistadors Spanish soldiers and explorers

Moctezuma II Aztec ruler who mistook Cortés for a god, leading to the Aztec's downfall

Academic Vocabulary

motive reason for doing something

Section Summary

THE AZTECS BUILD AN EMPIRE

The first Aztecs were poor farmers from northern Mexico who migrated south. Other tribes had taken the good farmland, so the Aztecs settled on a swampy island in Lake Texcoco (tays-KOH-koh). In 1325, they began building their capital here.

War was key to the Aztecs' rise to power. The Aztec warriors conquered many towns and made the conquered people pay tributes of cotton, gold, or food. The Aztecs also controlled the trade network.

The Aztecs' power and wealth was most visible in the capital, Tenochtitlán (tay-NAWCH-teet-LAHN). The Aztecs built three **causeways** to connect the island to the shore and floating gardens on the lake. At its peak, Tenochtitlán had about 200,000 people. The city had temples, a palace, and a busy market.

LIFE IN THE EMPIRE

Aztec society had clearly defined social classes. The king was the most important person.

> **Where were the humble origins of the mighty Aztecs?**
> _____
> _____
> _____
> _____

> **What were the two key ways that the Aztecs became rich, even if they did not have their own farmland?**
> _____
> _____
> _____

Section 2, *continued*

He was in charge of law, trade, tribute, and warfare. The nobles, including tax collectors and judges, helped the king with his duties. Below the king and nobles were priests and warriors. Priests had great influence over Aztecs. Warriors were respected for conquering new lands. Below priests and warriors were merchants and artisans, and then farmers and laborers. Slaves were lowest in society.

> Underline the sentence that describes the responsibilities of the king.

The Aztecs believed that gods ruled all parts of life and sacrifice was necessary to keep the gods happy. In rituals priests cut themselves to give blood to the gods and sacrificed nearly 10,000 humans a year.

> Why were Aztec religious ceremonies so bloody?
> _____
> _____
> _____
> _____

The Aztecs studied astronomy. Their calendar was much like the Maya calendar. The Aztecs had a rich artistic tradition and their own writing system. They also had a strong oral tradition.

CORTÉS CONQUERS THE AZTECS

In 1519 Spanish explorer **Hernán Cortés** (er-NAHN kawr-TAYS) led soldiers called **conquistadors** into Mexico. Their **motives** were to seek gold, claim land, and spread their religion. The Aztec ruler, **Moctezuma II** (MAWK-tay-SOO-mah), thought Cortés was a god. Moctezuma sent Cortés many gifts, including gold. Wanting more gold, Cortés took Moctezuma prisoner. Enraged, the Aztecs attacked the Spanish. They drove the Spanish out of the city, but Moctezuma was killed.

To defeat the Aztecs, the Spanish allied with tribes who resented the Aztec rulers. Together they used guns and rode horses. The Spanish also carried diseases like smallpox that killed many Aztecs. In 1521 the Spanish conquered Tenochtitlán. This brought the Aztec empire to an end.

> What factors contributed to the Spanish's defeat of the Aztecs?
> _____
> _____
> _____
> _____

CHALLENGE ACTIVITY

Critical Thinking: Drawing Inferences What do you think about Hernán Cortés and his actions toward the Aztecs? Write a one-page paper defending your opinion. Give examples to support your opinion.

Interactive Reader and Study Guide

The Early Americas

MAIN IDEAS

1. The Incas created an empire with a strong central government in South America.
2. Life in the Inca Empire was influenced by social structure and religion; the Incas made great cultural achievements.
3. Francisco Pizarro conquered the Incas and took control of the region in 1537.

Key Terms and People

Pachacuti ruler who expanded the Inca Empire in the mid-1400s

Quechua the language of the Incas

masonry stonework

Atahualpa the last Inca ruler

Francisco Pizarro Spanish conquistador leader who conquered the Incas

Academic Vocabulary

distribute to divide among a group of people

Section Summary

THE INCAS CREATE AN EMPIRE

While the Aztecs rose in Mesoamerica, the Incas were building an empire in South America. The Incas began as a small tribe high in the Andes. They built their capital, Cuzco, in modern-day Peru. In the mid-1400s, the ruler **Pachacuti** (pah-chah-KOO-tee) led the Incas to expand their territory. By the early 1500s, the Inca Empire stretched from northern Ecuador to central Chile.

To rule this empire of 12 million people, the Incas formed a strong central government. The Incas replaced local leaders of conquered areas with new people loyal to the Inca government. The Incas established an official language, **Quechua** (KE-chuh-wuh). The Incas paid taxes in the form of labor. This labor tax system was called the *mita* (MEE-tah). There were no merchants or markets.

> On what continent did the Incas build their empire?
>
> _____
>
> _____

> Where did the Inca tribe originate?
>
> _____
>
> _____

Instead, government officials would **distribute** goods collected through the *mita*.

> How did Incas get food, clothing and other goods?
> _____
> _____

LIFE IN THE INCA EMPIRE

Inca society had two main social classes. The king, priests, and government officials were the upper class. The upper class lived in Cuzco and did not pay the labor tax. The lower class included farmers, artisans, and servants. Most Incas were farmers. They could not own more goods than they needed.

The Inca religion was based on the belief that Inca rulers were related to the sun god and never really died. Inca ceremonies often included sacrifice of llamas, cloth, or food. They also believed certain natural landforms had magical powers.

> Incas believed their rulers were related to whom?
> _____
> _____

Incas are known for their **masonry**, or stonework. They built massive buildings and a network of roads. Inca artisans made beautiful pottery, jewelry, and textiles. The Incas had no written language. Instead, they kept records with cords and passed down stories and songs orally.

> The Incas excelled in the use of what building material?
> _____
> _____

PIZARRO CONQUERS THE INCAS

There was a civil war between an Inca ruler's two sons, **Atahualpa** (ah-tah-WAHL-pah) and Huáscar (WAHS-kahr). Atahualpa won, but the war had weakened the Inca army. On his way to be crowned king, Atahualpa heard that conquistadors led by **Francisco Pizarro** were in Peru. When Atahualpa came to meet with them, the Spanish captured him. They attacked and killed thousands of Inca soldiers. The Incas brought gold and silver to offer for Atahualpa's return. But instead the Spanish killed him. The Spanish defeated the Incas and ruled their lands for the next 300 years.

CHALLENGE ACTIVITY

Critical Thinking: Drawing Inferences The Incas used labor as a form of currency. What are the advantages and disadvantages of this type of economic system? Write a brief essay explaining your answer.

Interactive Reader and Study Guide

The Early Middle Ages

CHAPTER SUMMARY

The need for lords to protect their land	led to	
	led to	**knights maintaining an honorable code of behavior**
Feudalism	led to	**people's lives bound together by honor and duty**
Self-sufficient manors	led to	

COMPREHENSION AND CRITICAL THINKING

Use the answers to the following questions to fill in the graphic organizer above.

1. Explain How did the lord of a manor protect his land?

_____

_____

2. Identify Cause and Effect What kept a knight from abusing his power?

_____

_____

3. Evaluate How did an economic system of land and service, rather than money, impact people's lives?

_____

_____

4. Draw a Conclusion How was manor life different than town and city life?

_____

_____

The Early Middle Ages

MAIN IDEAS

1. The physical features of Europe vary widely from region to region.
2. Geography has shaped life in Europe, including where and how people live.

Key Terms and People

Eurasia the large landmass that includes Europe and Asia

topography the shape and elevation of the land in a region

Section Summary

THE PHYSICAL FEATURES OF EUROPE

Europe is a small continent, but it is very diverse. Many different landforms, water features, and climates can be found there. Although we call Europe a continent, it is part of **Eurasia**, a large landmass that includes both Europe and Asia.

Europe's **topography**, the shape and elevation of the land, varies widely from place to place. Southern Europe is very mountainous, with some of the world's highest mountains in the Alps. As you travel north, the land gets flat. Northern Europe was once covered in thick forests.

Most of Europe's rivers are in the north. Farther north, the land gets rugged and hilly again, though not as high as the mountains in the south. Many peninsulas jut out from Europe, creating a long and jagged coastline. The climate is hotter and drier in the south, and gets progressively colder as you move north.

> Why is Europe considered to be part of Eurasia?
>
> _____
> _____
> _____

> What is the highest mountain range in Europe?
>
> _____
> _____

GEOGRAPHY SHAPES LIFE

Not surprisingly, with this variety of topography and climate, life in early Europe was different depending upon where you lived. In southern Europe, most people lived on coastal plains or in river valleys where the land was flat enough to farm.

People grew crops like grapes and olives that could grow on mountainsides and also survive the region's dry summers. High in the mountains, where the land was too steep or rocky to farm, people raised sheep and goats.

Because southern Europe has a long coastline with numerous peninsulas, many people turned to the sea for food and transportation. Societies that lived in southern Europe often became great traders and seafarers.

Most people in northern Europe lived much farther from the sea than people in southern Europe did. They still had access to the sea, however, through northern Europe's many rivers. Because rivers were an easy means of transportation, many towns grew up along them. These rivers also sometimes provided protection for cities.

In the fields around cities, farmers took advantage of northern Europe's rich soils to grow all sorts of crops. These fields were excellent farmlands, but the flat land also created an easy route for invaders to follow. No mountains blocked people's access to northern Europe. As a result, the region was frequently invaded.

> List two reasons why grapes and olives are ideal crops for southern Europe.
> _____
> _____
> _____
> _____

> List two reasons why Northern Europe was frequently invaded.
> _____
> _____
> _____
> _____

CHALLENGE ACTIVITY

Critical Thinking: Drawing Inferences Where would you have preferred to live in Europe during the Middle Ages, if you had your choice? Write a short letter to a family member explaining what daily life is like in the area you choose and why you like it there.

The Early Middle Ages

Section 2

> **MAIN IDEAS**
> 1. Christianity spread to northern Europe through the work of missionaries and monks.
> 2. The Franks, led by Charlemagne, created a huge Christian empire and brought together scholars from around Europe.
> 3. Invaders threatened much of Europe in the 700s and 800s.

Key Terms and People

Middle Ages the period lasting from about 500 to about 1500

medieval another name for the Middle Ages

Saint Patrick Christian missionary credited with converting Ireland to Christianity

monks religious men who lived apart from society in isolated communities

monasteries communities of monks

Saint Benedict monk responsible for creating the Benedictine rule, a code prescribing a monk's behavior

Charlemagne warrior and king who led the Franks in building a huge empire

Section Summary

CHRISTIANITY SPREADS TO NORTHERN EUROPE

Europe was a dangerous place during Rome's long collapse. Without the Roman government, Europe had no central authority to keep order. Various groups from the north and east moved into former Roman lands, creating their own states and making their own kings. These kings often fought among themselves. As a result, by the early 500s Europe was divided into many small kingdoms. This marked the beginning of the **Middle Ages,** or **medieval** period.

At the beginning of the Middle Ages, most of the kingdoms of northern Europe were not Christian. Christianity was common only in places that had been part of the Roman Empire, such as Italy and

> List three reasons why Europe was so dangerous around the year 500.
> _____
> _____
> _____

> Why is the period between about 500 and about 1500 called the Middle Ages?
> _____
> _____

Spain. As time passed, Christianity slowly spread farther north, largely through the efforts of two groups of Christians—monks and missionaries.

The pope sent missionaries to northern Europe, hoping that Christianity would make Europe a safer place. Missionaries converted much of Germany, France, and Britain. One of the earliest missionaries, **Saint Patrick**, was an English Christian who took it upon himself to convert Ireland. Unlike missionaries **monks** lived apart from society in isolated communities, praying, working, and meditating. Communities of monks, or **monasteries**, were built all over Europe in the Middle Ages. Most monks followed a strict set of rules created in the early 500s by **Saint Benedict**.

> **Did the pope send Saint Patrick to Ireland?**
> _____
> _____

THE FRANKS BUILD AN EMPIRE

In the 500s a powerful group called the Franks conquered Gaul, the region we now call France. Under a ruler named Clovis, the Franks became Christian and created one of the strongest kingdoms in Europe. The Franks reached their greatest power during the 700s under **Charlemagne** (SHAHR-luh-mayn). At its height Charlemagne's empire reached from France into modern Germany, Austria, Italy, and northern Spain. Religious scholarship flourished in Charlemagne's time.

> **Who established Christianity among the Franks?**
> _____
> _____

INVADERS THREATEN EUROPE

While Charlemagne was building his empire, Europe was being attacked on all sides by invaders. The most fearsome were the swift and vicious attacks of the Vikings from Scandinavia.

> **Why do you think the Vikings are still so vividly remembered in our culture today?**
> _____
> _____
> _____
> _____

CHALLENGE ACTIVITY

Critical Thinking: Drawing Inferences The life of a monk in the Middle Ages was strict and without luxuries. Why would someone want to become a monk? Write a letter from the point of view of someone who wishes to join a monastery, explaining your decision to live the life of a monk.

The Early Middle Ages

MAIN IDEAS

1. Feudalism governed how knights and nobles dealt with each other.
2. Feudalism spread through much of Europe.
3. The manor system dominated Europe's economy.
4. Towns and trade grew and helped end the feudal system.

Key Terms and People

knights warriors who fought on horseback

vassal a knight who agrees to protect and serve a lord in exchange for land

feudalism the system that governs the relationship between lords and vassals

William the Conqueror French noble who conquered England and spread feudalism

manor large estate owned by a knight or lord

serfs workers who were tied to the land on which they lived

Eleanor of Aquitaine powerful French noblewoman who became queen of France and England

Section Summary

FEUDALISM GOVERNS KNIGHTS AND NOBLES

After Charlemagne's time, raids on Europe from the north and east intensified. The Frankish kings were unable to defend their empire. Nobles had to defend their own lands. Many nobles began to rule their lands as independent territories. These nobles needed soldiers. They gave **knights**, warriors who fought on horseback, land in exchange for military service. A noble who gave land to a knight was called a lord, while the knight was called a **vassal**. The system that governed the promises between lords and vassals is called **feudalism**.

Lords and vassals had responsibilities to each other. A lord had to send help if an enemy attacked a vassal. A lord had to be fair or vassals could break

> Why did many nobles become rulers of their own lands?
>
> _____
> _____
> _____

all ties with him. Vassals had to fight at a lord's command. They also had to house and feed a lord if he visited and sometimes pay him money.

List two responsibilities of a vassal toward a lord.

_____
_____
_____

FEUDALISM SPREADS

Frankish knights introduced feudalism into northern Italy, Spain, and Germany. From Germany, knights carried feudalism into eastern Europe. Feudalism reached Britain when **William the Conqueror** invaded and made himself king of England.

Who brought feudalism to eastern Europe?

_____
_____

THE MANOR SYSTEM

An estate owned by a knight or lord was called a **manor**. As fighters, knights had no time to work in the fields. Most peasants owned no land but needed to grow food to live. So knights allowed peasants to live and farm land on their estates. In return the peasants, or **serfs**, had to give the knights food or other payment. Skilled craftsman also lived and worked on the manor, which provided everything people needed.

What group supported the work of skilled craftsmen under feudalism?

_____
_____

Women in the Middle Ages had fewer rights than men, but they still played important roles in society. Some women, like **Eleanor of Aquitaine**, even became politically powerful.

TOWNS AND TRADE GROW

Most people lived in manors during the Middle Ages, but as Europe's population grew so did the size and number of towns and cities. The invention of the plough and increased trade eventually led to the decline of feudalism as people had more opportunities to make a living.

Why do you think people left the manors for the towns and cities?

_____
_____
_____
_____

CHALLENGE ACTIVITY

Critical Thinking: Drawing Inferences During the Middle Ages the ability for a person to better their lot depended upon where they started out in life. Research the options for advancement for the following people: the lord of the manor, lady of the manor, a vassal, a peasant, and a serf. 5

Section 4

> **MAIN IDEAS**
> 1. Feudal societies shared common elements in Europe and Japan.
> 2. Europe and Japan differed in their cultural elements such as religion and art.

Key Terms and People

chivalry code of honorable behavior for European knights

haiku short poems, with only three lines and 17 syllables, that usually describe nature themes

Section Summary

FEUDAL SOCIETIES SHARE COMMON ELEMENTS

Feudalism was not unique to Europe. You may have noticed a connection between the lords and vassals of Europe and, half a world away, the samurai and the daimyo of Japan. But how similar were the two societies?

Both knights and samurai were paid in land, rather than in money, and had peasants work the land for them. Both collected part of the crop yield in return for allowing the peasants to farm on their property. Both kinds of warriors promised to serve and fight for their nobles. In exchange for the land, both lords and daimyo expected their warriors to behave with honor and loyalty. The Japanese code of behavior for a samurai was called Bushido. A similar code of honorable behavior for European knights was called **chivalry**.

> How were knights, or vassals, and samurai paid for their military service?
> _____
> _____

> Underline the names of the two codes of honor that ruled behavior for the knights and samurai.

EUROPE AND JAPAN DIFFER

Still, there were many differences between the two cultures. Perhaps the main difference was expressed through religion. Although religion was important to both groups, the religious concepts were different. The Europeans were mostly Christians, while the Japanese had blended the naturalistic Shinto religion, where everything has a spirit, with Buddhism and Confucianism. Religion strongly influences the way people look at life and ultimately how they act.

The differences in religion appear in the art of the two cultures. In Europe most art of the Middle Ages showed Christian religious themes. Painting and sculpture represented scenes from the Bible or male and female saints. Poems and stories often taught people how to live or tried to inspire them with the lives of great Christians.

> **What is the main subject of most European medieval art?**
> _____
> _____

The art of Japan, on the other hand, expressed mostly natural scenes. Paintings of nature were common, and people designed and built beautiful gardens. The simple wooden architecture of a house was designed to blend into nature, rather than stand out. Japanese literature also celebrated nature. For example, Japanese poets in the 1600s created **haiku**, short poems of three lines and 17 syllables that often describe scenes of nature.

> **Write a haiku.**
> _____
> _____
> _____
> _____

Still, it is remarkable that similar systems of feudalism developed at the same time in two completely different cultures, located so far from each other. While feudalism has faded, it still impacts the life and culture of these two different regions today.

CHALLENGE ACTIVITY

Critical Thinking: Drawing Inferences How do you think religion influences your modern outlook and the people around you? Think hard about this concept. Even if you do not hold religious beliefs yourself, religion is a system of thought that influences how you view life and how you act. Write a brief essay discussing how your thoughts and attitudes on religion reflect the way you view the world.

The Later Middle Ages

CHAPTER SUMMARY

The rise of Christianity	led to	an increase in the political power of the church.
The Black Death	led to	the demise of the manor system.
The Magna Carta	led to	a new set of rights founding modern democracy.
Challenges to church authority	led to	persecution of Jews and other non-Christians.

COMPREHENSION AND CRITICAL THINKING

Use information from the graphic organizer and from the following pages to answer the following questions.

1. **Explain** Name one reason why the church became more politically powerful in the Later Middle Ages?

_____

2. **Identify Cause and Effect** How did the Black Death cause the end of the manor system?

_____

3. **Evaluate** Who wrote the Magna Carta? Why is it important to history?

_____

4. **Draw a Conclusion** Why do you think the rise of Christianity led to increased intolerance of Jews and other non-Christians?

_____

_____

The Later Middle Ages

Section 1

MAIN IDEAS

1. Popes and kings ruled Europe as spiritual and political leaders.
2. Popes fought for power, leading to a permanent split within the church.
3. Kings and popes clashed over some issues.

Key Terms and People

excommunicate casting an offender out of the church

Pope Gregory VII pope who excommunicated Emperor Henry IV

Emperor Henry IV Holy Roman ruler who challenged Pope Gregory VII

Section Summary

POPES AND KINGS RULE EUROPE

In the early Middle Ages, great nobles and their knights held most of the political power. As time passed this power began to shift to two types of leaders, popes and kings. The pope had great spiritual power. The kings had political power. Together, the pope and the kings controlled most of European society.

The pope was the head of the Christian Church. Since nearly everyone in the Middle Ages belonged to this church, the pope had great power. Christians believed that the pope was God's representative on earth. Because the pope was seen as God's representative, it was his duty to decide what the church would teach. From time to time, a pope would write a letter called a bull to explain a religious teaching or outline a church policy.

It was also the pope's duty to decide when someone was acting against the church. For the most serious offenses, the pope could choose to **excommunicate**, or cast out, an offender from the church. This much power often put the pope in direct conflict with the kings.

> **Name two of the pope's responsibilities as leader of the Christian church.**
>
> _____
> _____
> _____
> _____

> **Why do you think people feared the pope's ability to excommunicate them?**
>
> _____
> _____
> _____
> _____

Interactive Reader and Study Guide

Section 1, *continued*

In 1000 Europe was divided into many states that were ruled by kings. Many of the kings did not have much power. But the kings of England, France, and the Holy Roman Empire held a lot of power. In France and England, the throne was inherited through family. The Holy Roman Empire got its name because the empire existed with the pope's approval. In the Holy Roman Empire, the nobles elected the emperor. The pope settled any disagreements among the nobles.

> Underline how emperors were selected in France and England. Now, circle how an emperor was selected in the Holy Roman Empire.

POPES FIGHT FOR POWER

The popes of Western Europe tried to assert their authority over the bishops of Eastern Europe. The bishops of Eastern Europe did not want to answer to the pope. Pope Leo IX excommunicated the bishop of Constantinople when the bishop would not recognize the pope's authority. This caused a permanent split in the church between the Eastern Orthodox Church and the Roman Catholic Church.

> What event caused a permanent split in the church?
> _____
> _____
> _____
> _____

KINGS AND POPES CLASH

Popes also argued with kings, particularly over the king's right to select bishops. A dispute arose when **Pope Gregory VII** did not like a bishop chosen by Holy Roman Emperor **Henry IV**. Henry tried to remove the pope from office. The pope excommunicated Henry. Henry had to beg for the pope's forgiveness to remain in power. After their deaths, a compromise was ultimately struck. From then on, the pope would select religious officials, but religious officals must obey the emperor.

> During the lifetimes of Gregory and Henry, who would you say won their battle of wills?
> _____
> _____

CHALLENGE ACTIVITY

Critical Thinking: Drawing Inferences Would you have rather been a pope or a king during the Middle Ages? Write a one-page paper defending your answer.

The Later Middle Ages

Section 2

MAIN IDEAS
1. The pope called on Crusaders to invade the Holy Land.
2. Despite some initial success, the later Crusades failed.
3. The Crusades changed Europe forever.

Key Terms and People

Crusades a long series of wars fought between Christians and Muslims over control of Palestine

Holy Land the European name for Palestine, the region where Jesus had lived

Pope Urban II head of the Roman Catholic Church who started the Crusades

King Richard I English king who led the third, ill-fated Crusade to seize Palestine

Saladin Turkish leader of the Muslim forces that prevented England from taking Palestine

Section Summary

CRUSADERS INVADE THE HOLY LAND

The **Crusades** were a long series of wars between Christians and Muslims in Southwest Asia. The Europeans fought the Muslims to retake Palestine. Christians call the region the **Holy Land** because it was where Jesus had lived, preached, and died.

For many years Palestine had been ruled by Muslims. In general, the Muslims did not bother Christians who visited the region. In the late 1000s, however, a new group of Turkish Muslims captured the city of Jerusalem. Pilgrims returning to Europe said that these Turks had attacked them.

Before long the Turks began to raid the Byzantine Empire. The Byzantine emperor asked **Pope Urban II** of the Roman Catholic Church for help. Although the Byzantines were Eastern Orthodox Christians and not Roman Catholic, the pope agreed to help.

> **Why did Christians call Palestine the "Holy Land?"**
> _____
> _____
> _____

> **Circle the name of the person who made the call to arms that led to the Crusades.**

Interactive Reader and Study Guide

Pope Urban called on Christians to retake the Holy Land from the Muslim Turks. Crusaders from all over Europe flocked to France to prepare to fight. Many peasants set out on the First Crusade. The Crusaders used the holy war as an excuse to kill many Jews along the way to Palestine. Some Christians at the time blamed the Jews for the death of Jesus. The peasant Crusaders were defeated by the professional Turk army. However, the nobles and knights were able to capture Palestine and set up four kingdoms there.

> **Do you think the reason given for killing Jews was a mask for racial discrimination? Why or why not?**
> _____
> _____
> _____
> _____

LATER CRUSADES FAIL

Within 50 years the Muslims had started taking land back from the Christians. The Europeans launched more Crusades, but these invasions ended in defeat and heavy losses for the Christians. The Third Crusade started as a group effort between the German, French, and English kings. But only **King Richard I** of England stayed on to fight: His opponent was the brilliant Turkish leader **Saladin**. Eventually, King Richard left Palestine, which was still under Muslim control. By 1291 Muslims had taken back Palestine. The Crusades were over.

> **Circle the name of the European and Turkish leaders fighting in the Third Crusade.**

CRUSADES CHANGE EUROPE

The Crusades increased trade between Europe and Asia. In some cases, the Crusades increased the power of the kings. But the main impact of the wars was divisive. The Crusades hurt the trust European Jews had developed with Christians. The Crusades also caused a major split between the Muslim and Christian worlds. Those tensions are still felt today.

> **What do you think was the main impact the Crusades had on the world?**
> _____
> _____
> _____
> _____

CHALLENGE ACTIVITY

Critical Thinking: Drawing Inferences Were the Crusades justified? Using what you now know about the impact the Crusades continue to have on our society today, write a brief position paper stating your opinion. Be sure to list facts and examples to support your point of view.

The Later Middle Ages

MAIN IDEAS

1. The Christian Church shaped society and politics in medieval Europe.
2. Orders of monks and friars did not like the church's political nature.
3. Church leaders helped build the first universities in Europe.
4. The church influenced the arts in medieval Europe.

Key Terms and People

clergy church officials

religious order group of people who dedicate their lives to religion and follow common rules

Francis of Assisi founder of the Franciscan order

friars members of religious orders who lived and worked among the general public

Thomas Aquinas philosopher who showed how religious faith and reason could co-exist

natural law Thomas Aquinas's concept that God created a law that governed how the world operated

Section Summary

THE CHURCH SHAPES SOCIETY AND POLITICS

The **clergy** were very influential in medieval European culture and politics. For many people in the European Middle Ages, life revolved around the local church. Religious ceremonies like baptisms and weddings were key events in people's lives. Some people made pilgrimages, or journeys to religious locations.

The church owned a lot of land in Europe because many people left their property to the church when they died. In this way the church became a major feudal lord. Church officials often became political advisors to local rulers.

> List two key events in a person's life during the Middle Ages in which the local church was closely involved
>
> _____
> _____
> _____

MONKS AND FRIARS

Some people thought that the church was becoming too involved with politics. The monks of Cluny, France, established a new **religious order**. They dedicated their lives to religion with common rules. Other new orders followed. Women created their own religious communities in convents. Most monks lived apart from society, but two new religious orders developed for those who wanted to live and teach among people. These were the Dominicans, started by Dominic de Guzmán, and the Franciscans, started by **Francis of Assisi**. The members of these orders were called **friars**.

> Underline the sentence that explains why the monks of Cluny established a new religious order.

> How were the Dominicans and Franciscans different than the orders who lived in monasteries?
>
> _____
> _____
> _____
> _____

UNIVERSITIES ARE BUILT

Europe's first universities were built by the church. Religion, law, medicine, and philosophy were taught. Scholars wanted to establish a connection between religious faith and intellectual reason. The Dominican friar **Thomas Aquinas** wrote a reasoned argument for the existence of God. He also developed a philosophical system called **natural law** to show how God had ordered the world.

> Do you think it is necessary to be able to prove the existence of God? Why or why not?
>
> _____
> _____
> _____
> _____

THE CHURCH AND THE ARTS

The great Gothic cathedrals of late medieval Europe are among the most beautiful of all architectural achievements. Their spires and high ceilings and colorful stained glass windows are all designed to bring people closer to God. Everything inside the church, from the walls to the clergy's robes to the books used, were also works of art.

> Why do you think so much medieval European art was made for the church?
>
> _____
> _____
> _____
> _____

CHALLENGE ACTIVITY

Critical Thinking: Drawing Inferences Which medieval religious people do you agree with the most—those who became involved in politics, the monks who left society, or the friars who believed in working among the people? Write a one-page paper defending your views.

Interactive Reader and Study Guide

MAIN IDEAS

1. Magna Carta caused changes in England's government and legal system.
2. The Hundred Years' War led to political changes in England and France.
3. The Black Death, which swept through Europe in the Middle Ages, led to social changes.

Key Terms and People

Magna Carta document written by English nobles and signed by King John listing rights the king could not ignore

Parliament lawmaking body that governs England

Hundred Years' War long-standing conflict between England and France during the 1300s and 1400s

Joan of Arc teenage peasant girl who rallied the French troops and turned the tide of the Hundred Years' War

Black Death deadly plague that killed millions of Europeans between 1347 and 1351

Section Summary

MAGNA CARTA CAUSES CHANGE IN ENGLAND

In 1215 a group of English nobles decided to force the king to respect their rights. They made King John approve a document listing rights the king could not ignore. This document was called the **Magna Carta**, or "Great Charter." Among these rights was that no one could be kept in jail without reason, and even the king must obey the law. This charter became a key principle of English government and an important step in the development of democracy.

The Magna Carta led to more changes. Faced with war and financial troubles, the kings turned to a council of nobles for advice and money. Before long, the council developed into **Parliament**, the lawmaking body that still governs England today.

Why do you think the agreement between King John and the nobles was called the "great charter?"

_____

_____

_____

_____

Who made up the original British Parliament?

_____

_____

THE HUNDRED YEARS' WAR

In Europe, kings were not giving up their power easily, but other events forced political change. A major event was the **Hundred Years' War**, a long conflict between England and France. The war started when the English king tried to take control of France's throne. England invaded France and won many key battles until a teenage peasant girl, **Joan of Arc**, rallied the French troops. The English caught and killed Joan, but the French eventually won the war. In England, the war helped increase the power of Parliament because the king needed Parliament's approval to raise money to pay for the war. In France, the king's power grew after the war.

> **Why was Joan of Arc's feat truly remarkable? (List one of many possible reasons.)**
>
> _____
> _____
> _____
> _____

THE BLACK DEATH

During the Hundred Years' War an even greater crisis arose. This crisis was the **Black Death**, a deadly plague that swept through Europe between 1347 and 1351. The plague originally came from central and eastern Asia. Traders unknowingly brought rats carrying the disease to Mediterranean ports. From there it quickly swept throughout much of Europe. Fleas that fed on infected rats passed on the plague to people.

Some historians think the Black Death killed a third of Europe's population—perhaps 25 million people. This caused sweeping changes all over Europe. The old manor system, already weakened by the growth of cities, collapsed. Plague survivors found their skills in demand and charged more for their labor. Instead of working for the rich, peasants now had other job opportunities.

> **Underline the estimated number of victims of the Black Death.**

> **How did the Black Death ultimately benefit the survivors who lived on the manors?**
>
> _____
> _____
> _____
> _____

CHALLENGE ACTIVITY

Critical Thinking: Drawing Inferences Many events during the later Middle Ages impacted the way we live today. Take one event discussed in this chapter and write a one-page paper explaining how our lives might be different if this event had *not* occurred.

The Later Middle Ages

MAIN IDEAS

1. The church reacted to challengers by punishing people who opposed its teachings.
2. Christians fought Moors in Spain and Portugal in an effort to drive all Muslims out of Europe.
3. Jews faced discrimination across Europe in the Middle Ages.

Key Terms and People

heresy religious ideas that oppose accepted church teachings

Reconquista Christian efforts to retake Spain from the Muslim Moors

King Ferdinand Aragon prince who married Isabella of Castile to rule a united Spain

Queen Isabella Castilian princess who ruled Spain with her husband, Ferdinand of Aragon

Spanish Inquisition organization of priests charged with seeking out and punishing non-Christians

Section Summary

THE CHURCH REACTS TO CHALLENGERS

By around 1100, some Christians in Europe felt that the clergy were more concerned with money and land than with God. Others did not agree with the church's ideas. They began to preach their own ideas about religion.

Religious ideas that oppose church teachings are called **heresy**. Church officials sent priests and friars throughout Europe to find people who might be heretics. Most of these priests and friars tried to be fair, but some were not. Some tortured people until they confessed, even if they were innocent. Most people found guilty in these trials were fined or put in prison. Some, however, were put to death.

In the early 1200s, Pope Innocent III called for a crusade against heretics in southern France.

> Why do you think the church in late medieval Europe was so threatened by heresy?
>
> _____
> _____
> _____

> Do you think it was wise of the church authorities to leave the trials of heretics in the hands of individual priests and friars? Why or why not?
>
> _____
> _____
> _____

Interactive Reader and Study Guide

He encouraged the king and his knights to rid their country of heretics. The result was a bloody struggle that lasted about 20 years, destroying towns and cities and costing thousands of lives.

CHRISTIANS FIGHT THE MOORS

In Spain, the reign of the Muslim Moors collapsed in the 1000s. Christian kingdoms in Spain started a war to drive out the Muslims. They called their war **Reconquista** (reh-kahn-KEES-tuh), or reconquest. The kingdom of Castile was the first to free itself of Muslim rule. Portugal and Aragon soon followed. Castile and Aragon became united by the marriage of two royals, **King Ferdinand** of Aragon and **Queen Isabella** of Castile. Their union created the modern country of Spain. Portugal remained independent. In addition to banning Islam, Spain required all Jews to convert to Christianity or leave.

> What was the Reconquista?
> _____
> _____
> _____

Ferdinand and Isabella created the **Spanish Inquisition**, an organization of priests that looked for and punished non-Christians. The inquisition executed about 2,000 people in Spain and almost 1,400 more in Portugal.

> How many people in both Portugal and Spain died at the hands of the Spanish Inquisition?
> _____
> _____

JEWS FACE DISCRIMINATION

Spain's treatment of Jews spurred a more wide-scale attack on Jews. It had become common among many Christians to blame all Jews for the persecution and death of Jesus. Some people even blamed the Jews for the Black Death. In many kingdoms, Jews were driven out by angry mobs, and sometimes by the kings themselves. They had to flee from their homes or die.

> Name two things that some medieval Europeans blamed on the Jews.
> _____
> _____

CHALLENGE ACTIVITY

Critical Thinking: Drawing Inferences It is easy to see now that this period in history gave rise to intolerance and injustice for non-Christians. What could have led people to support such extreme and measures? Write a paper explaining how you think the church might have justified its methods.

The Renaissance and Reformation

CHAPTER SUMMARY

Increased trade with Asia	*led* to	
Wealth and love of art and education	*led* to	**the Renaissance.**
The printing press and universities	*led* to	
Martin Luther's protest	*led* to	**the Protestant Reformation.**
Protestant Reformation	*led* to	
The Council of Trent	*led* to	**the Catholic Reformation.**
Formation of new orders such as the Jesuits	*led* to	

COMPREHENSION AND CRITICAL THINKING

Use information from the graphic organizer to answer the following questions.

1. Explain Why did Italian cities lead the way as centers of learning?

_____

_____

2. Identify Cause and Effect How did the printing press help the Renaissance?

_____

_____

3. Make Inferences Why did the Lutherans form their own church?

_____

_____

4. Draw a Conclusion What impacts of the Catholic Reformation can we still see in the world today?

_____

_____

The Renaissance and Reformation

> **MAIN IDEAS**
> 1. Increased trade with Asia brought wealth to Italian cities, leading to the Renaissance.
> 2. Italian writers and artists contributed great works during the Renaissance.

Key Terms and People

Marco Polo European explorer who traveled through Asia in the 1200s

Renaissance period following the Middle Ages, characterized by renewed interest in Greek and Roman culture and an emphasis on secular rather than religious matters

humanism emphasis on human value and achievement

Dante Alighieri Italian poet who wrote *The Divine Comedy*

Niccolo Machiavelli political philosopher who wrote *The Prince*

Michelangelo master artist who painted the ceiling of the Vatican's Sistine Chapel

Leonardo da Vinci master inventor, engineer, and artist who painted the Mona Lisa

Academic Vocabulary

classical referring to the cultures of ancient Greece or Rome

Section Summary

TRADE WITH ASIA

Despite the Black Death's terrible death toll, the disease did not harm farmland, buildings, ships, machines, or gold. Survivors used these things to raise more food or make new products. Europe's economy began to grow. Some new products from the east appeared in markets. Traders brought these new goods across the Silk Road, a caravan route from Europe to China that had fallen into disuse. In the 1200s, the Mongols re-opened the Silk Road.

A traveler named **Marco Polo** spent 20 years in Asia. He wrote a book that rekindled an interest in the Far East. The book inspired traders to seek Asian goods.

By the 1300s Florence, Genoa, Milan, and Venice had become major trading centers in Italy.

> **Name one good result that came from the otherwise terrible Black Death.**
> _____
> _____
> _____

> **Why do you think the land route to China was called the Silk Road?**
> _____
> _____
> _____

Interactive Reader and Study Guide

These cities also were manufacturing centers. They made many specialized products. Venice and Genoa were port cities. Huge ships brought goods from Asia into their harbors.

Florence developed a banking system used all over Europe. The richest bankers were the Medici family. In Italian cities, rich families controlled the government. By 1434 Cosimo de Medici (KOH-zee-moh day MED-I-chee) ruled Florence. He wanted to make Florence a center of art, literature, and culture. This love of art and education was key to the **Renaissance**, which means "rebirth." The Renaissance followed the Middle Ages.

> Who usually controlled the Italian cities during this time period?
> _____
> _____

ITALIAN WRITERS AND ARTISTS

In the Middle Ages, most thinkers in Europe devoted themselves to religious study. In the Renaissance, people began to study poetry, history, and art. These subjects are part of the humanities. This emphasis on human achievement was called **humanism**. This led to a renewed interest in the **classical** writings of the Greeks and Romans.

> How was education in the Renaissance different than education during the Middle Ages?
> _____
> _____
> _____
> _____

Dante Alighieri (DAHN-tay ahl-eeg-YEH-ree) was an early Italian Renaissance writer. He wrote in Italian, the language of the common people, rather than in Latin. A later writer, **Niccolo Machiavelli** (neek-koh-LOH mahk-yah-VEL-lee), advised leaders on how they should rule in his book, *The Prince*.

> In what language did Dante Alighieri write?
> _____
> _____

A Renaissance person is one who does everything well. Two men best embodied this ideal. **Michelangelo** (mee-kay-LAHN-jay-loh) had many talents. He designed buildings, wrote poetry, made sculptures, and was a master painter. **Leonardo da Vinci** was another master in the arts. But he also was an architect, inventor, engineer, and mapmaker.

CHALLENGE ACTIVITY

Critical Thinking: Drawing Inferences Why do you think beauty and education were so important to the Medici family of Florence? Write a short paper explaining your answer.

The Renaissance and Reformation

MAIN IDEAS

1. During the Renaissance, advances in science and education were made.
2. New ideas from the Renaissance spread across Europe through the development of paper, printing, and new universities.

Key Terms and People

Petrarch Renaissance poet and scholar who helped change education

Johann Gutenberg German inventor of a printing press with movable type

Christian humanism combination of humanism and Christianity

Desiderius Erasmus priest and Christian humanist who critiqued corrupt clergy

Albrecht Dürer German painter who is also known for his block printing

Miguel de Cervantes Spanish writer of *Don Quixote*, a novel that mocked medieval habits and customs

William Shakespeare English dramatist and poet inspired by the Renaissance

Academic Vocabulary

affect to change of influence

Section Summary

ADVANCES IN SCIENCE AND EDUCATION

Renaissance scientists used math to make advances in fields such as engineering and architecture. They also discovered that the earth moves around the sun. There also were dramatic changes in education. Students began to study the humanities. History became very important. An early Renaissance scholar, **Petrarch** (PE-trahrk), was a champion of studying history. His ideas would **affect** education for many years.

> How was education in the Renaissance different than education during the Middle Ages?
>
> _____
> _____
> _____
> _____

THE SPREAD OF NEW IDEAS

Travelers and artists helped spread Renaissance ideas throughout Europe. The development of printing was a major revolution. For the first time, thousands of people could read books.

Section 2, *continued*

Papermaking came from China to the Middle East and from there to Europe. European factories were making paper by the 1300s. Then in the mid-1400s, a German named **Johann Gutenberg** (GOOT-uhn-berk) developed a printing press that used movable type. Using this method an entire page could be printed at once.

Scholars from around the world came to Italy to study. Humanist universities opened all over Europe. Women were not allowed to study in universities, but often they were educated at home.

> The Bible was the first book printed using Gutenberg's movable type. Why do you think that is?
> _____
> _____
> _____

THE NORTHERN RENAISSANCE

Scholars of northern Europe changed some Renaissance concepts. They often applied humanism to religious topics. They believed that human beings were valuable for their own sake, and the church should treat people better. They called for church reform. This combination of humanism with religion is called **Christian humanism**. A Dutch priest, **Desiderius Erasmus** (des-i-DEER-ee-uhs i-RAZ-mus), criticized corrupt clergy.

Northern artists also embraced realism. However, their people did not look like Greek Gods but were realistic, with physical flaws. German artist **Albrecht Dürer** (AWL-brekt DYUR-uhr) showed objects in great detail. He is known for his prints.

> Circle the name of a famous northern Renaissance painter who drew in a realistic style.

LITERATURE BEYOND ITALY

Like Dante, writers in other countries wrote in their native languages. In Spain, **Miguel de Cervantes** (mee-GEL day ser-VAHN-tays) wrote *Don Quixote* (kee-HOH-tay). In this book Cervantes poked fun at the romantic tales of the Middle Ages. The Renaissance also inspired the great English playwright and poet **William Shakespeare**.

> Why do you think Cervantes made fun of the ideas of the Middle Ages?
> _____
> _____
> _____

CHALLENGE ACTIVITY

Critical Thinking: Drawing Inferences How did the northern Europeans build upon Renaissance ideas? Write a paragraph using specific examples.

Interactive Reader and Study Guide

The Renaissance and Reformation

MAIN IDEAS

1. Martin Luther and other reformers called for change in the Catholic Church, but eventually broke away from the church.
2. The Catholic Reformation developed in the 1500s in response to the spread of Protestantism.
3. The political impact of the Reformation included wars between Protestants and Catholics and a new interest in self-government.

Key Terms and People

Reformation reform movement against the Roman Catholic Church

Martin Luther priest who criticized the church abuses and started the Reformation

Protestants those who protested against the Catholic Church

John Calvin reformer who taught that common people should have a say in church policy

Catholic Reformation the effort to reform the Catholic Church from within

Jesuits religious order founded to serve the pope and spread Catholic teachings

federalism sharing of power between national and local governments

Academic Vocabulary

agreement a decision reached by two or more people or groups

Section Summary

REFORMERS CALL FOR CHANGE

By the late Renaissance people began complaining about the Catholic Church. Many people thought the church was too rich. Some thought the priests were not religious. Many objected to the church's sale of indulgences. This led to the **Reformation**.

In 1517 a priest named **Martin Luther** called for reform. He nailed a list of 95 complaints to a church door in Germany. Luther was excommunicated and ordered to leave the empire. His ideas led to a split in the church. Those who protested against the Catholic Church were known as **Protestants**. Another reformer was **John Calvin**. His teachings included predestination—the idea that God knew who would be saved.

"Reformation" is a noun. Upon what verb is it built?

_____

_____

Define "Protestant."

_____

_____

_____

_____

THE CATHOLIC REFORMATION

The effort to reform the Catholic Church from within is called the **Catholic Reformation**. Catholic leaders worked to strengthen the church.

Catholic leaders met at the Council of Trent to discuss church reforms. The council made new rules for clergy. They rejected Protestant ideas. To win back support, Catholic reformers created new religious orders in southern Europe in the 1500s. One such order was the **Jesuits**. Rather than change the church, many Catholics decided to dedicate their lives to helping it grow. Missionaries spread Catholism around the world.

> Underline the name for efforts to reform the Catholic Church from within.

THE POLITICAL IMPACT

The Reformation left Europe divided. Most of northern Europe became Protestant. Most of southern Europe stayed Catholic. The Holy Roman Empire became a patchwork of small kingdoms. Some were Catholic and some were Protestant. Many conflicts arose because of this division.

In France, most people remained Catholic. The king outlawed the Protestants, called Huguenots (HYOO-guh-nahts). After decades of war between the Catholics and Huguenots, religious freedom was granted to most of France. The Holy Roman Empire fared no better. After the Thirty Years' War, Europe's rulers reached an **agreement**. It allowed rulers to decide the religion of their countries.

The Reformation led to social and political change. Most people had little to say in governing the Catholic Church. But in Protestant churches, each congregation made its own rules. National rulers began to share power with local governments. This system was called **federalism**. As a result, more people began to question authority.

> Which part of Europe became predominantly Protestant in the span of merely 100 years?
>
> _____
>
> _____

> How did religious reform led to political reform?
>
> _____
>
> _____
>
> _____
>
> _____

CHALLENGE ACTIVITY

Critical Thinking: Drawing Inferences What is the most important change from the Reformation that still impacts society today? Explain.

Interactive Reader and Study Guide

Science and Exploration

CHAPTER SUMMARY

Cause	Effect
Henry the Navigator builds school for sailors	Portugal becomes an early leader in exploration
Columbus discovers America	Questioning of old authorities
Vasco da Gama sails around Africa	New trade routes open to India
Copernican theory of a sun-centered solar system	Conflict of science and religion
Conquistadors defeat Incas and Aztecs	Spain rules much of the Americas
Mercantilism; triangle trade among Europe, Africa, and the Americas	Development of mining and plantations; exploitation of Africans and Native Americans
English and Dutch develop trade routes and banks	Shift of economic power in Europe
Success of science and reason	Democratic ideas gain favor; changing governments; conflict with the church
Demand for manufactured goods	Birth of capitalism

COMPREHENSION AND CRITICAL THINKING

Use information from the graphic organizer to answer the following questions.

1. **Identify Cause and Effect** Explain why the Catholic Church might have been threatened by the advances in both science and exploration.

_____

2. **Draw a Conclusion** What changes in society and politics were contributed to by the Scientific Revolution?

_____

_____

3. **Make Inferences** Why do you think Europeans prohibited trade among different American colonies founded by different countries?

_____

_____

4. **Contrast** How are capitalism and mercantilism alike? How do they differ?

_____

Science and Exploration

MAIN IDEAS

1. The Scientific Revolution marked the birth of modern science.

2. The discoveries and inventions of the Scientific Revolution helped scientists study the natural world.

3. The Scientific Revolution had broad effects on society, changing ideas about the physical world, human behavior, and religion.

Key Terms and People

Scientific Revolution series of events that led to the birth of modern science

theories explanations developed by scientists to explain observable facts

Ptolemy Greek astronomer whose work was based on observation and logic

Nicolaus Copernicus Polish astronomer who theorized that the planets orbit the sun

Johannes Kepler German astronomer who proved that planets' orbits are elliptical

Galileo Galilei Italian scientist and astronomer who tested his theories in experiments

Sir Isaac Newton English scientist who discovered laws of motion and of gravity

scientific method step-by-step procedure for performing experiments or research

Academic Vocabulary

logical reasoned, well thought out

principles basic beliefs, rules, or laws

Section Summary

THE BIRTH OF MODERN SCIENCE

The series of events that led to the birth of modern science is called the **Scientific Revolution**. It took place in Europe from roughly 1540 to 1700. Before this time, learned people relied on authorities—the ancient Greeks or the Catholic Church—for information about the world. Afterward they relied on observation and **logical** thinking.

Science is a specific way of gaining knowledge. Scientists identify facts by observation. Then they develop **theories** to explain facts. Theories must be tested. Science had its roots in ancient Greece. Aristotle and **Ptolemy** studied astronomy, logic, and

> Underline the two sentences that explain the basic method of science.

> What was so revolutionary about the Scientific Revolution?
>
> _____
> _____
> _____
> _____

Interactive Reader and Study Guide

geography. These thinkers were rationalists, people who looked at the world in a rational way.

DISCOVERIES AND INVENTIONS

In 1492 Columbus found a new continent. Greek thinkers never knew it existed. Scholars began to question authorities for the first time.

Ptolemy thought that the planets moved around the earth. Polish astronomer **Nicolaus Copernicus** disagreed with him. Copernicus thought the planets orbited the sun. **Johannes Kepler** proved that the planets orbit the sun in oval-shaped orbits. **Galileo Galilei** was the first person to study the sky with a telescope. **Sir Isaac Newton** was one of the greatest scientists. He developed theories of light, gravity, and motion. His theories have been proven so many times that they have become laws.

Scientists were helped by the microscope, the thermometer, and the barometer. They used these new inventions to observe the world more precisely.

> Why do you think Columbus's discovery of the New World cast doubt on the writings of ancient authorities?
>
> _____
> _____
> _____
> _____

> How did inventions help scientists?
>
> _____
> _____
> _____

EFFECTS ON SOCIETY

Francis Bacon and René Descartes encouraged the use of orderly experiments and clear reasoning. Their ideas led to the **scientific method**. The scientific method is a step-by-step procedure for doing scientific research. It involves observation and experimentation—the main **principles** of modern science.

Science had a great impact on society and politics. People recognized that logic could solve many human problems. Political problems could be solved by changing government. Democratic ideas gained favor. The advances of science also brought conflict. Church leaders tried to force scientists to reject findings that opposed the church's teachings.

> Why did applying the scientific model to human behavior lead to the idea that people are equal?
>
> _____
> _____
> _____

CHALLENGE ACTIVITY

Critical Thinking: Drawing Inferences Write a one-page paper describing a world without rationalist ideas. How would people think, feel, and react? How would they understand the world around them?

Science and Exploration

MAIN IDEAS

1. Europeans had a desire and opportunity to explore in the 1400s and 1500s.
2. Portuguese and Spanish explorations led to discoveries of new trade routes, lands, and people.
3. English and French explorers claimed land in North America.

Key Terms and People

Henry the Navigator Portuguese prince who started a sailing school and funded many expeditions

Vasco da Gama first explorer to sail safely around Africa to India

Christopher Columbus Italian explorer who accidentally discovered the Americas while searching for a shorter route to Asia

Ferdinand Magellan Portuguese navigator who first circumnavigated the globe

circumnavigate to go all the way around

Sir Francis Drake famous English pirate who robbed Spanish ships in the Americas

Spanish Armada huge fleet of Spanish ships defeated and wrecked while preparing to attack England in 1588

Section Summary

DESIRE AND OPPORTUNITY TO EXPLORE

Europeans began a new age of exploration in the 1400s. Advances in navigational tools, cartography, and shipbuilding spurred their interest in travel. Explorers set off in search of new trade routes to Asia. They wanted to find rare spices, to spread Christianity, and to discover new lands and people.

> List four motivations that drove European explorers during the 1400s and 1500s.
>
> _____
> _____
> _____
> _____

PORTUGUESE AND SPANISH EXPLORATIONS

Henry the Navigator helped make Portugal a great success on the seas. Henry built an observatory and a navigation school for sailors. He funded many sailing voyages. With Henry's help, a sailor named **Vasco da Gama** became the first person to sail safely around Africa to India.

Christopher Columbus was Italian, but he offered his services to Spain. He thought he could reach Asia

> Henry the Navigator never left Portugal. Why was he so influential in early Portuguese explorations?
>
> _____
> _____
> _____
> _____

Interactive Reader and Study Guide

by heading west across the Atlantic. His voyage led to the accidental discovery of the Americas. **Ferdinand Magellan**, a Portuguese navigator sailing for Spain, set out to **circumnavigate** the globe. Magellan was killed before the end of the trip, but his crew did become the first to go all the way around the globe.

After Columbus, the Spanish conquistadors sailed to the Americas in the early 1500s. With better weapons, they conquered the Incas and Aztecs. Spain soon ruled much of the Americas.

> Why did Columbus think he was sailing to Asia?
> _____
> _____
> _____

ENGLISH AND FRENCH IN AMERICA

As Portugal and Spain secured southern trade routes, France and England went north. Early journeys by explorers from both countries again confused North America with Asia, but they secured claims to the land. The famous pirate **Sir Francis Drake**, in the service of England, raided Spanish ships for their treasures. Spain retaliated by sending a fleet of ships, the **Spanish Armada**, to attack England in 1588. The English navy defeated the Armada with the help of a great storm at sea. Spanish sea power never recovered.

> How did English pirate Francis Drake contribute to Spain's loss of control over the sea?
> _____
> _____
> _____

A NEW EUROPEAN WORLD VIEW

The voyages of the 1400s and 1500s led to new and more accurate maps. These maps for the first time showed the entire world. Europeans saw a new world full of opportunity. They saw the potential for great wealth from colonies and trade. This ushered in a new period of European influence in the world.

CHALLENGE ACTIVITY

Critical Thinking: Drawing Inferences European explorers had to spend as much time raising money as they did sailing. Pretend that you are an explorer living in Spain, Portugal, France, or England during the 1400s. You need to convince a rich patron to pay for a sailing expedition. Write an argument in which you lay out the reasons and purpose for your trip.

Science and Exploration

MAIN IDEAS

1. Plants, animals, and ideas were exchanged among Europe, Asia, Africa, and the Americas.
2. In the 1600s and 1700s, new trading patterns developed and economic power shifted in Europe.
3. Market economies changed business in Europe.

Key Terms and People

plantations large farms

mercantilism trading system in which the government controls all economic activity

capitalism system in which individuals and private businesses run most industries

market economy system in which individuals decide what goods and services to buy

Section Summary

EXCHANGING PLANTS, ANIMALS, AND IDEAS

The New World (the Americas) exchanged plants, animals, and ideas with the Old World (Europe). This trade is called the Columbian Exchange. Europeans brought crops such as oranges, onions, lettuce, bananas, and sugarcane to the Americas. They also brought cows, goats, sheep, horses, pigs, and chickens. Europeans took home tomatoes, potatoes, beans, squash, and chocolate.

> Underline the names of the main crops that criss-crossed oceans in the Columbian Exchange.

Europeans introduced animals that made life and work easier. They brought horses for transportation, and the oxen and plough for farming. They also brought technologies such as guns, steel, and the wheel. New industries sprang up from these innovations, such as **plantations** and mining.

> What was new about the animals Europeans introduced in the Americas?
>
> _____
> _____

Sugarcane plantations and mines made a lot of money for Spain and Portugal. But these plantations were built on the backs of American Indians, who were forced into slave labor. Many Native Americans died as a result of harsh treatment and new diseases. Europeans then began to use Africans as slaves.

TRADE AND ECONOMIC POWER

Europeans saw the colonies as a way to get rich. This view of the colonies was part of an economic system called **mercantilism**. In this system, a government controls all economic activity in a country and its colonies. Mercantilism makes the government stronger and richer. To stay rich, each country tries to export more goods than it imports. Mercantilism was the main economic policy in Europe between 1500 and 1800.

A trade network called triangular trade began among Europe, Africa, and the Americas. Raw materials, manufactured goods, and slaves were traded. The Atlantic slave trade was a major part of the trade. Africans were crammed in ships without enough food or water and sold in the colonies.

Early on, Portugal and Spain benefited most from the mercantilism. But the English and Dutch developed new trade routes and established banks to shift power in their favor. The Dutch formed a company to trade directly with Asia. This helped them control many trading posts there. Economic power in Europe shifted.

> **How does a balance of trade benefit a country?**
> _____
> _____
> _____
> _____

> **Why do you think the trade among Europe, Africa and the Americas was called triangular trade?**
> _____
> _____
> _____

MARKET ECONOMIES

Increased wealth in Europe led to an increased demand for manufactured goods. People who came up with ways to increase the supply to meet the demand for goods created the basis of **capitalism**, a new economic system in which individuals and private business controlled most industries. This stimulates competition among manufacturers, and a **market economy**, in which individuals decide what goods and services they want to buy.

> **What stimulates competition in a capitalist economic system?**
> _____
> _____
> _____
> _____

CHALLENGE ACTIVITY

Critical Thinking: Drawing Inferences The roots of modern American cultures were built on the backs of African and American Indian slaves, who were treated as lesser people because of the color of their skin. In what ways does this racism still permeate the United States today?

Interactive Reader and Study Guide

Enlightenment and Revolution

CHAPTER SUMMARY

Event	Key People	Key Ideas
Enlightenment	Locke, _____, Rousseau	
American Revolution	Jefferson, _____	
French Revolution	King Louis XVI	

COMPREHENSION AND CRITICAL THINKING

Use the answers to the following questions to fill in the graphic organizer above.

1. Explain Which country was the first to abolish the divine right of kings?

_____

_____

2. Identify Cause and Effect Why were the American colonists unhappy with British rule?

_____

_____

3. Evaluate Why do you think the French took longer to form a democracy than England or America?

_____

_____

4. Draw a Conclusion What key ideas from the Enlightenment became founding principles in the English, American, and French declarations of human rights?

_____

_____

Enlightenment and Revolution

> **MAIN IDEAS**
> 1. The Enlightenment was also called the Age of Reason.
> 2. The Enlightenment's roots can be traced back to earlier ideas.
> 3. New ideas came mainly from French and British thinkers.

Key Terms and People

Enlightenment period in which people valued the use of reason as a guide to improving society

secular non-religious

Voltaire French writer who mocked government and religion

salon social gathering in which people discuss ideas

Mary Wollstonecraft British writer who championed women's rights

Section Summary

THE AGE OF REASON

The Scientific Revolution and the European exploration of the Americas caused a growing number of European scholars to challenge long-held beliefs about science, religion, and government. They believed the newly developed power of human reason could be used to increase knowledge, freedom, and happiness in the world. This use of reason to define politics and society defined a period called the **Enlightenment**.

> What do you think was "enlightened" about the Enlightenment?
> _____
> _____
> _____
> _____

THE ENLIGHTENMENT'S ROOTS

Enlightenment thinkers were influenced by the ideas of the ancient Greeks and Romans, the Christian Reformation, the Renaissance, and the Scientific Revolution. Greek philosophers like Aristotle believed there was a natural order to the world. This had been further expanded into the

> Underline the sentence that indicates how Aristotle inspired Enlightenment thinkers.

Interactive Reader and Study Guide

natural law envisioned by the Romans. Thomas Aquinas's demonstration that faith could be paired with reason caused people to challenge the church's authority. Renaissance thinkers had shifted emphasis from God to individual human achievement.

> **What institution had its authority undermined by the Enlightenment?**
> _____
> _____

Reformers like Martin Luther and scientists like Galileo had challenged the church's understanding of events. They found that church teaching was not always in line with reality or logic. All this led to a more **secular**, or non-religious, view of how society could be ordered.

> **Why did the Enlightenment cause a more secular movement?**
> _____
> _____

NEW IDEAS

French philosophers like **Voltaire** (vohl-TAYR) were openly outspoken in their disregard for the authority of the church and existing governments. He mocked both government and religion freely in his writings. He got in trouble for this, of course, and so spoke passionately against censorship.

Another Frenchman, Denis Diderot (dee-DROH), edited the first book to collect these ideas, a multivolume work called the *Encyclopedia*. It was banned by the king of France and the pope. People began to sponsor **salons**, social gatherings to discuss ideas.

Though women were still not considered equal to men, many women sponsored salons. British writer **Mary Wollstonecraft** argued in favor of women's rights.

> **In what country did the subject of women's rights first surface as a serious idea?**
> _____
> _____

CHALLENGE ACTIVITY

Critical Thinking: Drawing Inferences If you were to hold a salon today, what would the topics of discussion include? Have students in the classroom define important topics (e.g. war, racism, politics, poverty, teen pregnancy, etc.) and discuss ideas on how to resolve these issues. Remind your students that all ideas are equally valid, but students must defend their opinions with reasons, and be prepared for possible disagreement.

Enlightenment and Revolution

> **MAIN IDEAS**
> 1. The Enlightenment influenced some monarchies.
> 2. Enlightenment thinkers helped the growth of democratic ideas.
> 3. In America, the Enlightenment inspired a struggle for independence.

Key Terms and People

John Locke English philosopher who said government is a contract between ruler and the people

natural rights Locke's idea that every person has the right to life, liberty, and property

Charles-Louis Montesquieu French philosopher who said government should be divided into separate branches, each branch limiting the power of the other branch

Jean-Jacques Rousseau French writer who proposed the idea of popular sovereignty

popular sovereignty government that expresses the will of the people

Benjamin Franklin American philosopher, scientiest, and statesman who argued before the British Parliment for the repeal of extra taxes on colonists

Thomas Jefferson American statesman who proposed the idea of colonial independence

Academic Vocabulary

contract a binding legal agreement

Section Summary

ENLIGHTENMENT INFLUENCE ON MONARCHIES

In the 1600s most European monarchs thought they ruled by right imparted directly from God. The Enlightenment challenged this belief. It inspired some rulers to try to improve life for common people. These rulers were called enlightened despots. Although the enlightened despots made some improvements in their countires, many Enlightenment thinkers, began to consider the need for democracy.

> Look up the word "despot" in a dictionary and write the definition here:
> _____
> _____
> _____
> _____

DEMOCRATIC IDEAS

Three Enlightenment thinkers set the stage for modern democracy. English philosopher **John Locke** argued against a ruler's divine right, proposing instead that government should be based on a **contract** between the ruler and the people. He also said the government should have one goal: the peace, safety, and public good of the people. Locke said people had **natural rights** to life, liberty, and property.

French thinker **Charles-Louis Montesquieu** (mohn-te-SKYOO) expanded on these ideas, saying that government should be divided into separate branches, each one limiting the power of the other. Another Frenchman, **Jean-Jacques Rousseau** (roo-SOH), proposed the idea of **popular sovereignty**, that governments express the will of the people.

> What did John Locke believe was the only goal of a government?
> _____
> _____
> _____

> Underline Rousseau and Montesquieu's ideas about government.

THE ENLIGHTENMENT IN AMERICA

British colonists living in America were deeply moved by these ideas. When the British government began to chip away at what the colonists saw as their rights, they began to protest. They began by arguing against the extra taxes Britain imposed on colonists for certain products. American printer and scientist **Benjamin Franklin** traveled to London and argued successfully in Parliament for the repeal of these taxes. Franklin argued that the British government had no right to tax the colonists because the colonists had no representative in Parliment. Meanwhile, **Thomas Jefferson**, a scholar, scientist, and farmer, proposed the idea of independence for the colonies.

> Who were the two American colonists who took conscious action based on the ideas of Locke, Montesquieu, and Rousseau?
> _____
> _____
> _____

CHALLENGE ACTIVITY

Critical Thinking: Drawing Inferences Write up your own legal contract with your teacher about how to preserve the peace, safety, and public good in your classroom. Be very specific and thoughtful about the rules you choose. Remember, both sides need to follow rules.

Enlightenment and Revolution

Section 3

MAIN IDEAS

1. Revolution and reform changed the government of England.
2. Enlightenment ideas led to democracy in America.
3. The French Revolution caused major changes in France's government.

Key Terms and People

English Bill of Rights document that listed rights agreed on between British rulers, the Parliament, and the people in 1689

Declaration of Independence document declaring the colonie's independence form British rule in 1776

regime government in power

Declaration of the Rights of Man and of the Citizen document granting freedom of speech, the press, and religion for the French

Academic Vocabulary

ideals ideas or goals that people try to live up to

Section Summary

REVOLUTION AND REFORM IN ENGLAND

In England, the uneasy relationship been Parliament and the monarchy exploded into a civil war in 1642. A series of rulers took power before Parliament invited William of Orange to invade and overthrow the king in 1688. William took power, but only after agreeing to sign an **English Bill of Rights** for Parliament and the English people in 1689. William became king, but shared power with Parliment.

> When was the English Bill of Rights signed?
> _____
> _____

DEMOCRACY IN AMERICA

The English Bill of Rights did not apply to the American colonies. The colonies developed their own governing bodies, but were still subject to burdensome taxes and trade restrictions. Though

> Underline the phrase that indicates the main American grievances against English rule.

Section 3, continued

not all Americans wanted independence, everyone wanted more equitable treatment. When their protests were put down by British troops, the colonists organized militias to protect themselves. In 1776 Thomas Jefferson drafted the **Declaration of Independence**, announcing the colonies' independence from British rule.

The Declaration clearly expresses Enlightenment **ideals**. Britain eventually gave up the fight and recognized the independence of the colonies. A new government plan for the United States, in keeping with Montesquieu's idea about separate branches, was developed by James Madison and others.

> What general area of European thought underlay the push for independence in America??
> _____
> _____

> Circle the name of the person who drafted a new form of government for the United States of America.

THE FRENCH REVOLUTION

The American Revolution inspired the French to rebel against their own **regime**. Most commoners in France had no say in government at all, paying high taxes with virtually no rights. A National Assembly was formed to demand rights from King Louis XVI, but he refused to listen.

The French Revolution began in 1789. The king eventually agreed to rules similar to the English Bill of Rights and the American Declaration of Independence, called the **Declaration of the Rights of Man and the Citizen**. Still, Louis was eventually tried and executed. It took the French several years to develop a stable new government because the rage of the commoners, called the Reign of Terror, was hard to control. Eventually, France also installed a democratic system of government.

> Why were the commoners of France so outraged at the king?
> _____
> _____
> _____

> How did Louis XVI die?
> _____
> _____

CHALLENGE ACTIVITY

Critical Thinking: Drawing Inferences You are a revolutionary agitator, either in England, the British colonies in America, or in France. How would you inspire your neighbors and friends to join you in the fight? Develop a character and write a persuasive speech that is historically appropriate to the period. Depending on the country you choose, remember to mention the other country's revolutions whose ideas inspired your own.

Interactive Reader and Study Guide

Revolutions and Nations

CHAPTER SUMMARY

NATIONALISM
growth of nation states
pride in national identity
military buildup

INDUSTRIALISM
need for raw materials for production
need for markets for goods
growing middle class

IMPERIALISM
control of other regions
control of markets
spread of own culture

COMPREHENSION AND CRITICAL THINKING

Use information from the graphic organizer to answer the following questions.

1. Explain How did the need for raw materials and the growth of the middle class contribute to a new wave of imperialism?

_____

_____

2. Make Inferences The United States sent Commodore Matthew Perry to Japan to negotiate a trade treaty. Japan wanted to avoid foreign domination. How did Japan avoid becoming a colony?

_____

_____

3. Make Inferences The steam engine made it cheaper to distribute imported goods. How did the steam engine contribute to imperialism?

_____

_____

4. Make a Prediction How do you think the growth of national pride inside colonies would affect imperialism?

_____

_____

Revolutions and Nations

Section 1

MAIN IDEAS

1. During the Napoleonic Era, Napoleon conquered vast territories in Europe and spread reforms across the continent.

2. At the Congress of Vienna, European leaders tried to restore the old monarchies and ensure peace.

3. Inspired by revolutionary ideals in Europe, Latin American colonies began to win their independence.

Key Terms and People

Napoleon Bonaparte French general who became emperor

coup d'état forceful overthrow of a government

Klemens von Metternich Austrian prince who led the Congress of Vienna

conservatism movement to preserve the old social order and governments

liberalism movement for individual rights and liberties

Simon Bolívar a leader of South American independence movements

Academic Vocabulary

opposition the act of opposing or resisting

conflict an open clash between two opposing groups

Section Summary

THE NAPOLEONIC ERA

Napoleon Bonaparte became a hero in France after the French Revolution. In 1799 he took power in a **coup d'état**, the forceful overthrow of the government. While he was emperor, France controlled much of Europe. He improved the education and banking systems. Napoleon issued a set of laws that brought new freedoms to the French people. But he did not allow **opposition** to his rule.

Napoleon's rule ended after the British defeated his navy and Russia defeated his armies. European nations worked together to remove him from power. They forced him to leave France. After he returned with a new army, Napoleon was defeated by English forces at the Battle of Waterloo.

> Why do you think the new set of laws was known as the Napoleonic Code?
>
> _____
> _____
> _____
> _____

Interactive Reader and Study Guide

THE CONGRESS OF VIENNA

At the Congress of Vienna, European leaders met to write a peace settlement. Prince **Klemens von Metternich** of Austria led the meetings. France was forced to give back territories conquered by Napoleon. The shapes of the countries near France were changed to balance power in Europe. These changes were to ensure that no one power could threaten the rest of Europe.

These leaders opposed the ideals of the French Revolution. They preferred **conservatism** and the way things had been. They wanted the old system and old rulers to continue. **Liberalism**, which was built on individual rights, gained strength in the next few decades. Conservatives remained in control, but things had begun to change.

> What was the goal of the Congress of Vienna?
> _____
> _____
> _____
> _____

> Why do you think most of the European leaders were conservatives?
> _____
> _____
> _____

LATIN AMERICAN INDEPENDENCE

The ideals of the French Revolution crossed the Atlantic Ocean. They spread through the Caribbean and South America. Many colonies fought for their independence. In the French colony of Haiti, Toussaint L'Ouverture led a slave rebellion. The result was Haiti's independence. **Simon Bolívar** led the fight for independence across South America. By 1831 a dozen Latin American nations had won their freedom.

Bolívar tried to build peace on the continent. But the new nations fought over borders. There was also **conflict** between conservatives and liberals. Conservatives wanted the rich to control the new governments. Liberals wanted the people to vote for leaders. These conflicts caused many governments to be unstable. There were many changes of leaders as the governments rose and fell.

> What caused the new governments in Latin America to be unstable?
> _____
> _____
> _____
> _____

CHALLENGE ACTIVITY

Critical Thinking: Make Inferences Changes in government often occur as a result of conflict, such as the French Revolution. Why don't these changes always result from peaceful agreement between sides?

Revolutions and Nations

MAIN IDEAS

1. During the Industrial Revolution, new machines and methods dramatically changed the way that goods were produced.
2. Industrialization and the factory system brought a new way of life to Europe and America.

Key Terms and People

factory system a production system in which machines rapidly produce goods

laissez-faire an attitude that government should stay out of business matters

socialism a system in which businesses are owned by workers or the government

Karl Marx German philosopher who called for workers to unite against the capitalist system

Section Summary

NEW MACHINES AND METHODS

In the 1700s and 1800s, there were many new inventions and scientific discoveries. These advances changed the way people lived and worked. Factories grew. There were great strides in the way people communicated and in the ease of travel. This period was called the Industrial Revolution.

Machines did much of the work that had been done at home. They made manufacturing faster. The invention of the steam engine provided power for the machines and for trains and ships. The **factory system** used machines to rapidly produce large quantities of goods. Ships and trains delivered the goods to faraway markets faster than ever before.

Factories grew in the United States and Western Europe in the 1800s. The factory system was funded by capitalists. These were bankers and merchants who invested capital, or money. Because they provided the money, they did not want the government to control business. They wanted a **laissez-faire** (leh-say-FAR) attitude. In this approach, the government leaves business alone.

> **How did development of the steam engine help business?**
>
> _____
> _____
> _____

> **Why do you think that capitalists were able to convince the governments to stay out of business matters?**
>
> _____
> _____
> _____

Interactive Reader and Study Guide

At the same time, scientific research increased. Scientists found ways to prevent and cure diseases. Chemists and physicists made discoveries about the structure of atoms, the particles that make up everything. Many other fields of science, such as geology and psychology, advanced as well.

> **How did advances in science help the factory system grow?**
> _____
> _____
> _____
> _____

A NEW WAY OF LIFE

The Industrial Revolution changed the way that millions of people lived. Factories made goods faster. The people who had made products in the country no longer had a way to support themselves. They moved to the cities and took jobs in the new factories. Thus, cities quickly grew.

Factory workers worked long hours in dangerous and tiring jobs for low wages. Even children worked in the factories. In addition to the hard work, people in the cities had to endure crowding, crime, and pollution.

> **Underline the sentences that describe ways in which the Industrial Revolution made workers' lives harder.**

Some people wanted to replace the capitalist system. They hoped workers would be treated better in a socialist system. **Socialism** is a system in which the government or the workers own the businesses. German philosopher **Karl Marx** called for workers to unite and bring down capitalism.

> **What is the main difference between socialism and capitalism?**
> _____
> _____
> _____
> _____

The changes of the 1800s helped some people more than others. A middle class of people with good incomes grew. The middle class included factory managers, clerks, merchants, engineers, doctors, and other well-educated people. The upper and middle classes had time for the arts. There were two major trends in the arts. Romanticism stressed beauty, nature, emotions, and simpler times. Realism tried to show everyday life as it really was.

CHALLENGE ACTIVITY

Critical Thinking: Make Judgments Do you think that a socialist system would cure all of the problems caused by the Industrial Revolution? Write a one-page paper defending your opinion.

Revolutions and Nations

MAIN IDEAS

1. Nationalism sparked independence movements in Europe and the unification of Italy and Germany.
2. Colonial empires grew in the late 1800s as industrialism led to a new wave of imperialism.

Key Terms and People

nationalism devotion and loyalty to one's own country

nation-states self-governing countries of people with a common culture

Giuseppe Garibaldi Sicilian leader who helped unite Italy into a single country

Otto von Bismarck Prussian leader who developed a plan to unify Germany

imperialism control of a region or country by another country

Matthew Perry U.S. naval leader who negotiated a treaty with Japan

Academic Vocabulary

competition a contest between two rivals

Section Summary

NATIONALISM

In the 1800s the way goods were made changed. In addition, other important changes occurred. Now many people in the world were ruled by people from a different culture. As they grew tired of this situation, nationalism developed. **Nationalism** is a devotion and loyalty to one's own country. People wanted to rule themselves. They began to unite with others who shared their cultures, beliefs, and customs. They supported the idea of **nation-states**. These states are self-governing countries of people with a common culture and background.

In the early 1800s Italy was divided into many states. Each had a different ruler. As nationalism grew, many people in Italy wanted to unite into one country. Efforts to unite the country failed at first. Then **Giuseppe Garibaldi** and Camillo di Cavour

> What caused people to start thinking about nationalism and building their own nations?
>
> _____
> _____
> _____
> _____

> Why do you think it takes one or more strong leaders to get individual states to join into one nation-state?
>
> _____
> _____
> _____
> _____

Interactive Reader and Study Guide

Section 3, *continued*

each gained control of several Italian states. They joined their lands together into one kingdom.

Germany was also made of many small states in the 1800s. German nationalists grew stronger when Italy became united. **Otto von Bismarck** was the prime minister of the largest state, Prussia. He came up with a plan to unite Germany. He gained control of the northern states through war. When he waged war on France, the southern German states sided with Prussia. In 1871 the German Empire was declared. King Wilhem became emperor.

> How did Otto von Bismarck get smaller states to join with Prussia, without attacking them?
>
> _____
> _____
> _____

COLONIAL EMPIRES

As the European nation-states united, they wanted to grow in strength. One way to do this was to get colonies around the world. These new nations joined other European countries in **competition** for colonies. By controlling other regions of the world, they obtained raw materials for industry and markets for their goods.

> Underline the sentences that describe ways that nations can benefit from having an empire.

Imperialism is the control of one region or country by another country. The countries of Europe took over areas of Africa and Asia. They formed empires. Many imperialists felt that they were doing good for the people in the colonies, who they saw as less advanced.

The United States did not want Europe to build new colonies in the Americas. At the same time, the United States expanded west. It also gained control of the Phillipines, Puerto Rico, Hawaii, and part of Panama. The United States wanted to open up trade with Japan. They sent Commodore **Matthew Perry** to obtain a treaty with the Japanese. Japan was determined to avoid foreign domination so the country industrialized its economy and built its own empire.

> Why do you think the United States wanted to prevent European nations from establishing new colonies in the Americas?
>
> _____
> _____
> _____
> _____

CHALLENGE ACTIVITY

Critical Thinking: Evaluate France, Britain, and Spain were able to build an empire long before Italy and Germany. Why didn't Italian and German imperialism begin before the 1800s?

Interactive Reader and Study Guide

Global Challenges

CHAPTER SUMMARY

Major Conflicts of the 20th Century

	World War I	World War II	Cold War
When	1914–1918	1938–1945	1945–1991
Major Powers Involved	Germany, Austria-Hungary, France, Great Britain, Russia, United States	Germany, Italy, Japan, Great Britain, France, United States, Soviet Union	United States, Soviet Union
Underlying Causes	nationalism, imperialism, military buildup	world economic collapse, resentment of WWI treaty, rise of dictators	struggle for superpower influence, ideological differences
Major Changes Afterward	map of Europe redrawn, Russian Revolution	imperialism declined, communist vs. non-communist nations, rise of UN, superpowers defined	decline of communism, breakup of Soviet Union

COMPREHENSION AND CRITICAL THINKING

Use the information in the graphic organizer above to answer the following questions.

1. Identify Cause and Effect Which countries became superpowers as a result of World War II?

_____

2. Draw a Conclusion During what part of the 20th century was imperialism most widespread? In what ways did it contribute to the first global war?

_____

_____

3. Evaluate Why is the Cold War called a war, even though it did not have military combat like the world wars?

_____

_____

Global Challenges

MAIN IDEAS

1. The onset of World War I can be traced to nationalism, imperialism, and the buildup of military forces in Europe.
2. The Allies' victory over the Central Powers came soon after the United States entered the war.
3. The Treaty of Versailles changed the map of Europe and created resentment.
4. The Russian Revolution resulted in the world's first communist state.

Key Terms and People

communism a system in which the government controls all business and the economy
Vladimir Lenin Bolshevik leader who built support among workers and soldiers

Academic Vocabulary

defend to keep secure from danger

Section Summary

THE ONSET OF WAR

Nationalism and imperialism caused strong rivalries among the nations of Europe. Some countries were working to expand their power. Others were still ruled by other countries. As European nations began to build large armies, they started to fear one another. Nations formed alliances and promised to **defend** their allies if they were attacked.

In 1914 a Serbian nationalist killed the heir to the throne of Austria-Hungary. Austria-Hungary then declared war on Serbia. The alliances caused Europe to split into two warring sides. The Central Powers were led by Austria-Hungary and Germany. The Allies were led by Great Britain, France, and Russia. Countries worldwide joined the fight.

> Why do you think so many European countries built large armies in the early 1900s?
>
> _____
> _____
> _____
> _____

> Why did so many countries fight in World War I, even though the original conflict involved only two of them?
>
> _____
> _____
> _____
> _____

THE ALLIES' VICTORY

When Germany attacked France and Belgium, French and British troops stopped them near Paris.

Interactive Reader and Study Guide

Neither side gained an advantage for three years. Millions of people were killed by powerful new weapons. When Germany started using submarines to attack supply ships, the United States warned against attacking unarmed ships. Germany ignored the warning, and the United States joined the Allies. American troops gave the Allies an advantage. The Central Powers were defeated in 1918.

> Underline the sentences that explain why the United States became involved in a war in Europe.

THE TREATY OF VERSAILLES

The Allies met after the war at Versailles (ver-SI), near Paris, to discuss peace terms. U.S. President Woodrow Wilson suggested a plan to prevent more wars. The plan included a League of Nations, in which countries would work to solve problems peacefully. The Allies drew a new map of Europe. They created new nations and allowed nationalities to rule themselves. Germany had to reduce its army, give up its colonies, and pay for war damages. Because many people did not like the terms of the treaty, it set the stage for more conflict.

> What was the purpose of the League of Nations?
>
> _____
> _____
> _____
> _____

THE RUSSIAN REVOLUTION

World War I led to a revolution in Russia. Problems had been growing for decades. People turned against the government because of poverty, food shortages, and loss of lives in the war. The Bolsheviks, who supported communism, gained power. **Communism** is a system in which the government owns all business and controls the economy. **Vladimir Lenin**, the Bolshevik leader, gained support from workers and soldiers. He overthrew the government and built the world's first communist state, the Soviet Union.

> Why would people think that problems could be solved by changing to a different government?
>
> _____
> _____
> _____
> _____

CHALLENGE ACTIVITY

Critical Thinking: Make Inferences One result of the Treaty of Versailles was the creation of new nations out of parts of Russia, Germany, and Austria-Hungary. How could this have decreased European stability? Write a one-page paper explaining your answer.

Global Challenges

> **MAIN IDEAS**
> 1. Another global conflict, World War II, pitted the Allies against the Axis Powers from 1939 to 1945.
> 2. The results of World War II included a staggering loss of life and a new power struggle between the United States and the Soviet Union.

Key Terms and People

fascism a political philosophy based on nationalism and strong government

Allies Great Britain and France, and later the United States

Axis Powers Germany, Italy, and Japan

Holocaust an effort by the Nazis to exterminate the Jewish people

genocide the deliberate destruction of a people

Cold War a period of intense rivalry between superpowers without direct fighting

Section Summary

ANOTHER GLOBAL CONFLICT

After World War I many countries had deep economic and political problems. But then these problems grew worse. The Great Depression caused a severe economic slump around the globe.

In the crisis, people looked to strong leaders. In Japan the military took over. The dictator Joseph Stalin rose to power in the Soviet Union. Benito Mussolini came to power in Italy and Adolf Hitler became ruler of Germany. They found support with **fascism** (fa-shiz-um). Fascism is a political approach based on nationalism and a strong government.

Hitler was bitter about the effects of the Treaty of Versailles. He worked to rebuild German power. When Germany attacked Poland, the **Allies**—Great Britain and France—declared war on Germany. Germany formed an alliance with Italy and Japan. This group was known as the **Axis Powers**. After France fell to the German army in 1940, the British used their air force to resist the Germans. Meanwhile Germany attacked the Soviet Union.

> How did the economic problems after World War I help cause World War II?
> _____
> _____
> _____
> _____

> What action caused the Allies to declare war on Germany?
> _____
> _____
> _____
> _____

Interactive Reader and Study Guide

Japan attacked the United States at Pearl Harbor in 1941, and the U.S. joined the Allies. Battles were fought around the world using the most powerful weapons ever seen. In 1944 American and British troops landed in France and pushed toward Germany while Soviet troops attacked Germany from the east. Germany surrendered in May 1945. In order to bring the war in the Pacific to an end, the United States dropped two atomic bombs on Japan. Japan surrendered days later.

> Germany was vulnerable at the end of World War II because it was fighting a two-front war. What does this mean?
>
> _____
> _____
> _____
> _____

RESULTS OF THE WAR

World War II was the deadliest conflict in history. More than 22 million soldiers were killed. Another 34 million were injured. More than 30 million civilians were also killed.

Many of the civilian casualties were victims of the **Holocaust** (HO-luh-kost). This was an effort by the Nazis to exterminate the Jewish people. This act of **genocide** (JE-nuh-side), the deliberate destruction of a people, killed 6 million Jews. Millions of other people were also killed by the Nazis. Thousands of civilians were also killed in Japan when the atomic bombs were dropped.

> Underline the sentences that explain why the Holocaust is considered an act of genocide.

The war changed the power balance in the world. The United States and the Soviet Union became the two strongest nations. These two countries no longer trusted one another. There was a long period, called the **Cold War**, during which they had a tense rivalry but no direct fighting.

During the Cold War, the United States used economic aid to support its allies in western Europe. At the same time, the Soviet Union helped set up communist governments in Eastern Europe.

> Why was the tension between the United States and the Soviet Union called a Cold *War* if there was no direct fighting?
>
> _____
> _____
> _____
> _____

CHALLENGE ACTIVITY

Critical Thinking: Making Predictions How might World War II have been different if Japan had not decided to bomb the U.S. forces at Pearl Harbor? Write a short paper to explain your answer.

Global Challenges

> **MAIN IDEAS**
>
> 1. Colonialism came to an end after World War II, as countries in Asia, the Middle East, and Africa gained independence.
> 2. The Cold War ended with democracy on the rise and communism in retreat.
> 3. Worldwide terrorism has become a great threat to peace.
> 4. Global interdependence creates new opportunities and challenges for all of us today.

Key Terms and People

Mohandas Gandhi leader of the independence movement in India

ideologies systems of belief

Korean War North Korea and China against South Korea and United Nations troops, including those from the United States

Vietnam War North Vietnam against South Vietnam and the United States

Ronald Reagan U.S. president at the end of the Cold War

Mikhail Gorbachev Soviet leader at the end of the Cold War

terrorism use of violence to create fear and push for political change

Academic Vocabulary

neutral not engaged on either side

Section Summary

THE END OF COLONIALISM

After World War II the nations of Europe were weak. They could no longer hold their empires. In India **Mohandas Gandhi** led protests against British rule. India was Britain's most important colony. In the end, Britain split the colony into two parts, India and Pakistan, and granted each independence.

Nationalism grew in the decades after World War II. European countries lost colonies in Asia, the Middle East, and Africa. Some changes were peaceful and others were violent. As new nations formed, some made alliances with the United States or the Soviet Union. Others remained **neutral**.

> Why did the European nations have trouble keeping their colonies after World War II?
>
> _____
> _____
> _____
> _____

THE COLD WAR

The Cold War began as an arms race between the United States and the Soviet Union, and lasted for more than 40 years. Both sides knew that using nuclear weapons could destroy much of the world. The Cold War became a battle between **ideologies**, or systems of beliefs.

Much of the world was involved in the Cold War. Many countries were allied with the United States or the Soviet Union. Germany was divided into two parts. In Asia the Cold War was violent. The **Korean War** ended with no winner. The **Vietnam War**, between the North Vietnam and South Vietnam, ended with communism prevailing.

In the 1980s President **Ronald Reagan** expanded the U.S. military forces. The Soviet Union, led by **Mikhail Gorbachev**, had economic problems trying to keep up. The reform in Eastern Europe led to the fall of European communism. Soon after, the Soviet Union broke up into 15 countries.

> What were the two superpowers whose relationships defined how the Cold War developed?
>
> _____
>
> _____

> Underline the sentences that describe some effects of the Cold War on Asia.

WORLDWIDE TERRORISM

Many modern conflicts involve **terrorism**, the use of violence to create fear and push for political change. Terrorism has been a major tactic in Northern Ireland, Spain, South America, Africa, Asia, and the Middle East. Terrorist acts include shootings, bombings, kidnappings, and hijackings. Since the end of the Cold War, terrorism is the top threat to peace in the world.

> How does terrorism differ from conventional warfare as a way to create political change?
>
> _____
>
> _____
>
> _____
>
> _____

GLOBAL INTERDEPENDENCE

People all over the world are closer together now than at any time in history. Rapid changes in technology have led to a global economy. But there are both challenges and opportunities as countries try to work together.

CHALLENGE ACTIVITY

Critical Thinking: Evaluate How has the increase in terrorism affected your life? Consider, among other things, effects on travel and security.